ALSO BY STEVE BROUWER

Exporting the American Gospel (coauthor)

Conquest and Capitalism

SHARING THE PIE

SHARING THE PIE

A Citizen's Guide to Wealth and Power in America

STEVE BROUWER

ILLUSTRATIONS BY STEVE BRODNER

An Owl Book

HENRY HOLT AND COMPANY

NEW YORK

Henry Holt and Company, Inc.
Publishers since 1866
115 West 18th Street
New York, New York 10011

Henry Holt is a registered trademark of
Henry Holt and Company, Inc.

Library of Congress Cataloging-in-Publication data are available.
Brouwer, Steve, 1947–
Sharing the pie : a citizen's guide to wealth and power
in America / Steve Brouwer.
        p.   cm.
"An Owl book."
Includes bibliographical references and index.
ISBN 0-8050-5206-2 (pb : alk. paper)
1. United States—Economic conditions—1981–
2. United States—Social conditions—1980–
3. United States—Politics and government—1981–1989.
4. United States—Politics and government—1989–
        I. Title.
HC103.B783   1998   97-43523
338.973—dc21   CIP

Henry Holt books are available for special promotions and
premiums. For details contact: Director, Special Markets.

First Owl Books Edition 1998

Designed by Jessica Shatan

Printed in the United States of America
All first editions are printed on acid-free paper. ∞

            1   3   5   7   9   10   8   6   4   2

CONTENTS

PART IV

ACKNOWLEDGMENTS

Thanks to my wife, Susan D. Rose, who not only is a talented sociologist but is tolerant and supportive of my efforts to make the U.S. political economy comprehensible to the general reader. Thanks to many friends who encouraged me over the years and were willing to share their viewpoints and expertise in the fields of economics, history, politics, business, and labor.

Thanks to Rick Balkin, my agent, for realizing that we have returned to a time when a well-reasoned left perspective can find a readership in the United States. And to Steve Hubbell, my editor, and the other people at Henry Holt who have weighed in to help me with a difficult task: paring down a vast set of arguments and data to the essential ideas and concepts that this short book requires.

Thanks to numerous scholars who have diligently kept developing lucid analyses from a liberal to radical perspective. (Some of those who deserve mention are listed under suggested readings.) Their work—which often has not received the attention it deserves—has provided a solid foundation for understanding what is really going on in the United States during this extremely conservative time in our history.

And thanks to the many readers who have written to me over the past eight or nine years: professors who use the book in their classes; students who see prospects of changing the world; and an array of people—an electrician, a retired physician, a schoolteacher, a grape picker, a community organizer, a prison inmate, a homemaker, a businessman who can look beyond the marketplace—who are upset with the unfair and repressive elements that have crept into American society. Some of you have told me this was the first book on economics that you were able to comprehend. Which makes me feel like I'm doing my job.

And thanks to American working people, who labor hard and skillfully and receive too little in return. We live in a rich society that ought to be making it easier to earn a living, to raise a family, to care for our children and elderly relatives, and to enhance the quality of our schools and communities. It is in hopes of a brighter future for all Americans that this book is written.

SHARING THE PIE

SHARING THE PIE: AN INTRODUCTION

In the mid-1990s, the American people have constantly been told—by the President and the Congress, by the news media, and by the leaders of our corporations and banks—that our nation is in excellent economic health. As is the custom of all politicians during economic upturns, Bill Clinton has claimed credit for a booming stock market, a lower unemployment rate, and a manageable rate of inflation. In this moment of triumphalism, no one wanted to mention the single most striking feature of our economic and social landscape: the great gulf that exists, not just between rich and poor, but between the rich and everyone else. No amount of "bridge-building to the twenty-first century" (to quote the President's favorite phrase) can span a divide that increasingly separates the few who hold wealth and power from the majority of Americans.

When Clinton was first elected in 1992, many Americans hoped he would show the way toward reversing the distressing economic, social, and political trends of the 1980s. He had spoken eloquently about "feeling the pain" of working Americans who could not make ends meet, about ending the racial and ethnic bigotry that was creeping back into public life, and about acknowl-edging the shameful inability of the richest country on earth to provide basic health care for all of its citizens.

Four years later, all these manifestations of the earlier "progressive" Bill Clinton had disappeared. He had abandoned the fight for health care reform early in his first term, consigning an ever-increasing number of Americans—over 40 million—to a life without medical insurance. By mid-1996 Clinton's ideas on welfare "reform" were so close to those of the conservative Republican majority in Congress that he signed their bill to "end welfare as we know it." Rather than provide for decent employment, child care, and education for the poorest Americans (positions he had supported in 1992), Clinton decided that it was now politically accept-able to remove people—including millions of children—from the eligibility lists for family assistance payments, disability support, and food stamps. The *Wall Street Journal*, which never relented in its criticism of Clinton from a conservative perspective, neverthe-less had to admit its grudging admiration for the man who in 1996 mounted "the most right-wing campaign of any Democrat since Grover Cleveland."

In his bid for reelection, Clinton showed a

fondness for a vaguely worded agenda of how to restore the moral order in America. He recommended that V-chips be installed in televisions to help parents control the content of programming, and he touted the benefits of requiring children to wear uniforms to public schools. On substantial matters, the President fell closely in line with the programs sketched out by his fellow Southerners, the ultraconservative Republicans who headed up the Congress. The conservatives' Contract with America, while not entirely successful, did amount to a coherent program for contracting out the powers of government to private interests and expanding the opportunities of big business. Trent Lott, probably the most conservative Senate majority leader of the century, joined with House Speaker Newt Gingrich to guide the Republican Party sharply to the right.

Clinton, on the other hand, was not redirecting his party, but abandoning it. While his Democratic supporters claimed that the President had merely played the rhetorical game that was necessary to get himself reelected, there was little change in Clinton's rightward drift after he was inaugurated for a second term in 1997. His inaugural and State of the Union messages contained the same reassuring platitudes about building bridges but revealed no concrete plans about where he planned to take the United States in the next century.

Instead Clinton chose to take us back to the beginning of the twentieth century, to the issue that has animated the discourse of Republicans for over a hundred years: how to keep the taxes of the richest Americans as low as possible. When he negotiated the budget and tax bills of 1997, he readily granted the fondest wish of his predecessor, George Bush: another reduction in the capital gains tax. While the Republicans were

ready to settle for lowering the capital gains rate to 20 percent, Clinton's negotiators decided they could match that bid and beat it: a 20 percent rate for the first few years, and an 18 percent rate beginning in 2001. As for the rest of the tax structure, the President and Congress tacked together a number of small measures that did not threaten the status quo. Although Clinton had once spoken in favor of more spending on education, most of that spending came in the form of tax breaks to middle-class citizens who were already sending their children to college. He dared make only the weakest gesture toward a decent health care system, offering to aid about 5 million children with the proceeds of a new tax on tobacco, while 35 million other Americans would remain without protection.

Why had this happened? How had the leader of the Democratic Party moved so far rightward that he was now even more conservative than such Republican presidents as Dwight Eisenhower and Richard Nixon? One partial answer is that times had changed: we once again live in an era when economic and political conditions favor the accumulation of wealth and resources by the very rich. This first became obvious during the administration of Ronald Reagan, when the number of billionaires quadrupled, going from 13 to 52 between 1982 and 1988. This trend settled into a predictable pattern: the number of billionaires kept multiplying so fast that *Forbes* magazine was able to find 170 in 1997; most passed the billion-dollar mark during Clinton's first five years in office. Those who hoped a Democratic president would (or could) change the direction of the United States were sorely disappointed, for "Clintonomics," if there was such a thing, just kept us on the road toward increasing inequality.

For all his aspirations to be recalled as a friend of the middle class, Bill Clinton will most likely go down in history as the President who presided over the dismantling of the Welfare State. Whatever its weaknesses or imperfections, the Welfare State was conceived as a program of popular opposition to the destructive forces of capitalism. Although it was allowed to function actively and successfully for a relatively short time, from about 1935 to 1975, it represented the one time in U.S. history that most working people both participated in and benefited from the exercise of popular democracy. The government of the United States, like those of most nations in Western Europe, was expected to provide universal rights and protections to all members of society. In this way, ordinary citizens—as opposed to the elite classes that had previously controlled human societies—prospered as never before.

Bill Clinton did not have the power to prevent the demise of the Welfare State, so he meekly acceded to the inevitability of the triumph of big money over the remnants of popular democracy. Whether or not he was happy about this state of affairs hardly matters. Clinton and Robert Rubin, the secretary of treasury whom many regard as the second most powerful man in Washington, managed a nearly impossible task: they oversaw the most gigantic stock market boom in history at the same time that the U.S. economy enjoyed its slowest growth since the Great Depression of the 1930s.

It was unfortunate that Clinton was incapable of summoning the kind of language spoken by truly important Presidents at similar historical moments. Woodrow Wilson, a conservative Democrat who had pragmatic relations with Wall Street and often saw his more idealistic dreams go down to defeat, found the courage to tell Americans that "the masters of government of the United States are the combined capitalists and manufacturers of the United States." And Abraham Lincoln, who would later free the slaves from the most onerous conditions of forced labor, felt compelled to address the dignity of all working people in his inaugural statement of 1861. Like most American leaders then and now, he was the product of contradictory influences: his "log cabin," populist upbringing was offset by his eager service as lawyer for the railroad corporations that overran the prairie farmers in the 1850s. Still, he was not afraid of offending the rising contingent of the rich Eastern Establishment in his own Republican Party in his first message to Congress:

"Labor is prior to, and independent of, capital. Capital is only the fruit of labor, and could never have existed if labor had not first existed. Labor is the superior of capital, and deserves much the higher consideration."

It's hard to imagine Bill Clinton speaking or writing such words. This is an indictment of the times we live in more than of one individual who happens to be President, for most other major politicians would also choke on Lincoln's words.

When I wrote the first edition of this book, which appeared in 1988, I attempted to demonstrate that the rich, with the aid of the "Great Communicator," Ronald Reagan, were stealing the country blind and in so doing were setting the stage for the economic and social decline of the United States. The second edition, in 1992, showed how George Bush's administration avoided dealing with real problems as it promoted the welfare of our upper class and the corporations.

Now, as the 1990s are coming to an end, it is time for the Clinton administration to take its share of the blame. The first half of the 1990s was a period of such weak economic growth that distinguished economists and political analysts likened it to something worse than a recession, calling it a "never-ending recession," a "quiet depression," a "recession cum depression," and a "middle-class meltdown."[1] From 1990 through 1995, median family incomes and wages declined steadily, showing losses in five out of the six years, by far the worst performance in six decades. The annual economic growth rate from 1990 to 1995 was a dismal 1.7 percent a year, nearly as bad as the 0.8 percent growth rate of the 1930s. On one score, wages, the Great Depression may have been less depressing than the 1990s: average pay was 17 percent higher in 1939 than it was in 1930. Not so in the 1990s: by 1997 wages were 6 percent lower than in 1990, with no prospects of dramatic increases in pay before the new century arrived.[2]

While the stock market was still booming well into 1997, most Americans continued to worry about their shrinking or stagnant paychecks and the very real possibility that they would be "downsized." For average wage earners, the first four years of the Clinton administration had been no improvement on the Republican administrations that had preceded it.

Why is this so? For one thing, the flood of money into the coffers of the rich has produced a subsidiary overflow of record proportions that finds its way into the pockets of the leading politicians of both political parties. Partly for this reason, American citizens have heard a very narrow range of political discourse in the past twenty years: a far-right program from the Republicans and a patchwork of center-right policies (one can hardly call it a program) from the Democrats.

Both parties, in their steady slide to the right, have conceded control of our country to the large corporations and financial institutions that dominate economic and social activity and are the main repositories of individual wealth. Corporate capitalism, left more and more to its own devices, was able to promote patterns of private accumulation that made the 1980s and the 1990s the most unfair decades since the 1920s. This shift of wealth to the richest Americans has created unprecedented burdens for our society. Among them are huge amounts of private and public debt, greater levels of poverty and near-poverty, and a pattern of overspending on inessentials such as corporate mergers, military hardware, and luxury goods for the few. Meanwhile we have underfunded public infrastructure and technological research and failed to provide what all other highly industrialized societies offer their citizens: universal health care and quality education. We should not be surprised that the economies of Japan and Western Europe have surpassed us in many areas.

This book tells what went wrong in the last two decades of the twentieth century and provides powerful reasons for changing the course of our country as we begin the twenty-first century. Although it often feels satisfying to single out particular politicians, economic actors, or social leaders as deserving the blame for our predicament, we would do better to think about how the American political economy works. *Sharing the Pie* is an attempt to portray the economic problems and social inequalities of the United States in a way that the general reader can comprehend. There are many subjects discussed here that bear further elaboration, so the notes and the list of selected readings suggest where one might go for more in-depth source material.

If a society is in decline, we often notice

the symptoms first. Thus Part I of this book looks primarily at greed and unfairness: the hoarding of wealth by the rich; the shrinking of the middle-income strata of the working classes; the promotion of "well-to-do-fare" for the wealthiest citizens through changes in our tax system; and finally, the demonization and punishment of the poor.

Part II examines how the economy operates, focusing on the concentration of power in the biggest corporations and banks; it contrasts the gains at the top of the managerial class with the losses and humiliations suffered by average wage earners in the workplace. These trends are linked to the various ways in which our business structure has become wasteful, dishonest, and addicted to gambling with the nation's financial resources.

Part III reminds us that power does not rest on economic control alone, for we live within an unequal social structure that originated in the era of the nineteenth-century "Robber Barons." Although the patterns of class domination keep changing, they inevitably give rise to antidemocratic tendencies. Three political trends reflect the way a one-sided "class war" has been waged in American society over the past twenty-five years. First, government has acted as a willing accomplice of the wealthy in their massive plunder of public and private treasuries. Second, austerity for working people has been repeatedly put forth as the "new realism." And third, authority—that is, the authoritarianism exercised by government and corporations alike—has been promoted as a necessary element for enforcing discipline in our society.

Lest we end on too grim a note, Part IV of *Sharing the Pie* suggests that it is still possible for working people to assert their democratic rights and enjoy the fruits of industrialized society. The working and middle classes in other advanced capitalist countries have been effective at limiting the power of the corporate elite through the exercise of social democracy. We ought to do likewise, and very quickly, before the three forces that have put us in trouble—greed, austerity, and authoritarianism—continue to spread and to dominate the global arena. If we want to restore the health of our nation, we must use the power of the majority to challenge and curb the economic desires of the few.

1. Ravi Batra, *The Great American Deception*, New York: Wiley, 1997, p. 161. The economic experts, coming from different perspectives, were: Lawrence Hunter, Batra, John Kenneth Galbraith, and Peter G. Peterson.

2. Ibid., p. 4.

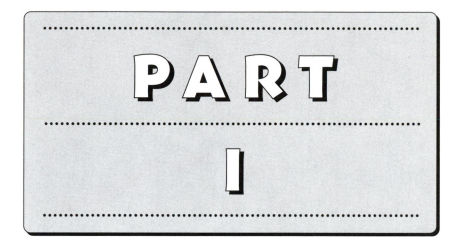

PART

I

SHARING
THE PIE

The distribution of wealth in the United States today is terribly unequal. The richest Americans, the top 1 percent, own almost half of the financial assets in our country. The affluent members of the upper middle class who make up the next 9 percent of the population own slightly more than one third of the wealth. That leaves only about one sixth to be divided among everyone else. A rich person, on average, has about 230 times more wealth than a member of the huge majority of Americans, the 90 percent who own very little at all. The pie is divided up like this:

OWNERSHIP OF FINANCIAL ASSETS[1]	
The Very Rich (1% of the Population)	46%
The Affluent (the Next 9%)	36%
The Rest of Us (90% of Americans)	18%

To no one's surprise, President Clinton did not brag about these statistics at the "Economic Summit" of the G-7 nations held in Denver in the summer of 1997. But he did try to claim that the U.S. economy was outperforming the rest of the world. The leaders of the other six large capitalist economies that make up the G-7—Germany, Japan, France, Italy, Britain, and Canada—did not agree, for they recognized the problems lurking behind the so-called good news that Clinton was trying to peddle.

First of all, the only momentous economic growth in the United States in the mid-1990s was in the stock market, which was fed by a long-term speculative binge that primarily benefited very rich investors, Wall Street traders, and the largest businesses. The profits of giant corporations jumped 58 percent from 1992 to 1997, but this increase was not accompanied by any gains in wages and salaries for ordinary workers. The number of decently paying corporate jobs was on the decline, even at the middle-management levels.

Clinton boasted that the large number of new jobs created in the United States was proof that our economy was strong. But more often than not these were lousy jobs characterized by low pay, bad working conditions, the loss of health insurance, and part-time or temporary status. They certainly were not the kinds of jobs that the other G-7 nations wanted to provide for their citizens. Although rising unemployment was an increasingly grave problem for these countries, their citizens were not so desperate that they were willing to accept the poverty-wage employment (under $7.28 per hour) that had become customary for 30 percent of the U.S. population.[2] There was a major weakness in the U.S. economy that presidential rhetoric could not hide: U.S. productivity growth had fallen steadily for almost thirty years.

ANNUAL GROWTH RATES OF U.S. PRODUCTIVITY BY DECADE[3]				
1950s	1960s	1970s	1980s	1990–95
2.7%	3.1%	1.9%	1.3%	1.2%

(Productivity grows when each working person is able to produce more goods or better-quality goods and services within an hour of work, thus producing greater value in a given amount of labor time. Rising productivity is the engine that creates wealth.)

In the other G-7 nations, productivity growth was also faltering compared with earlier decades, although it grew slightly faster, by 1.8 percent, than the U.S. rate in the 1980s and then fell to the same level, 1.2 percent, in the early 1990s. But in these countries the compensation of manufacturing workers grew considerably, 1.9 percent and 1.2 percent annually,[4] an amount that was commensurate with the productivity growth in both periods. In the United States, by contrast, manufacturing workers suffered an annual decrease in their compensation of 0.6 percent in the 1980s and realized no gain in the early 1990s. Only in the United States did the majority of working people find that the fruits of their toil were not passed along to them. Who, then, was reaping the benefits produced by the huge American economy?

Hogging the Pie

The United States is not the world leader in many economic categories these days. But we are still the champions at making a few people very rich. As you can see by the figures that begin this chapter, wealthy people are not just slightly richer than the rest of us—they are hogging the whole pie.

There are three ways we can look at the division of total individual net wealth (that is, all assets owned minus all kinds of debt). One way is to consider everything owned by every citizen:

TOTAL WEALTH OWNED[5]		
AVERAGE WEALTH PER HOUSEHOLD		GROUP SHARE OF ALL U.S. WEALTH
$9,000,000	The Very Rich (the top 1%)	37%
$950,000	The Affluent (the next 9%)	35%
$75,000*	The Rest of Us (the bottom 90%)	28%

*For the bottom 90%, most wealth consists of possessions—cars, household goods, and equity built up in homes—that are utilized in everyday life. Almost half of these people, the bottom 40%, have a net worth approaching zero, because their debts cancel out any property or assets they may own.

A second way to compare wealth is to look at ownership of financial assets (see page 12). By subtracting out the value of such things as automobiles, house furnishings, and residences, we get a truer measure of usable wealth, the kind of ownership that gives a person distinct advantages in a capitalist society. Because most people have invested more in household assets and cars than in financial holdings, the share of wealth held by the bottom 90 percent of the population falls to just 18 percent when only financial assets are considered. The share of the affluent upper-middle class stays about the same, but the share of the very rich, who own almost half of all financial assets, jumps up sharply to 46 percent.

There is a third way of looking at accumulated wealth that reveals even greater inequality. When we focus on the ownership of our economic system itself—the stocks and bonds of corporations, the privately held business assets, and the large trust funds and investment portfolios that are managed by banks—we find that total control is in the hands of the richest 1 percent.

CORPORATE AND BUSINESS ASSETS OWNED[6]				
	BUSINESS ASSETS	STOCKS	BONDS	TRUSTS
The Richest (1%)	61.6%	49.6	62.4	52.9
The Next 9%	29.5%	36.7	28.9	35.1
The Rest of Us (90%)	8.9%	13.6	8.7	12.0

This kind of wealth, which gives real economic power to a tiny fraction of our population, also reveals the truly undemocratic side of our society. Some scholars who carefully follow the patterns of ownership and financial control have found that the real wealth that translates into social and political power is held by a fraction of the very rich. In 1978 Maurice Zeitlin identified a group of 55,400 households, just 1/20th of 1 percent of the population, who owned 20 percent of all corporate stock, 66 percent of all state and local bonds, and 40 percent of all other bonds

and notes.[7] In the mid-1980s economist Lester Thurow reviewed the survey data for the richest four hundred individuals in the United States and eighty-two additional family groups who held extraordinary wealth. He estimated that through their ties to corporate ownership this tiny band of people had direct and indirect control over business assets amounting to more than $2 trillion, or "40% of all fixed nonresidential capital in the United States." With this kind of wealth, said Thurow, "it is hard to maintain the equality of influence that is the backbone of democracy."[8]

G. William Domhoff has argued convincingly that there is a core of wealthy people "who rule America," that they form a true upper class from which a minority gravitate toward prominent positions in business and government.[9] But this class is not stagnant. New people are always moving up to join the ranks of the very rich; occasionally an aggressive millionaire financier or entrepreneur attains billionaire status. Within the elite ranks are the people who manage the big corporations, those who hold high positions in the banks and law firms that simultaneously serve Wall Street and Washington, and those passively rich families who collect the dividends from the largest personal fortunes. All in all, these families not only control the majority of corporate wealth, but they also self-consciously nurture upper-class tastes and elite private education, as well as the next generation of financiers and presidential cabinet members.

The Billionaires Binge

Of course, there have always been some very rich people in the United States, and they have wielded tremendous political power. During the period between 1865 and 1929—

the era of the Robber Barons, the railroad trusts, and the oil monopolies—the richest citizens exercised unchallenged control over the economy and many other aspects of American life. Then, following the Great Depression and the economic reforms of the New Deal, ownership of wealth became more equal from the mid-1940s through the mid-1970s.[10] Millionaires had by no means disappeared, but the very rich held only about half as much of the nation's wealth as they had before the Depression. This trend reversed itself in the late 1970s as the wealthy reasserted their economic dominance and inequality accelerated rapidly. By the 1980s, the country's financial assets were being transferred to the rich at a phenomenal rate.

The analysis of Edward N. Wolff, professor of economics at New York University and the editor of the *Review of Income and Wealth*, demonstrated that the richest 1 percent gained control of 5.4 percent of the nation's financial assets in just six years, from 1983 to 1989[11]; this transfer of wealth was worth approximately $2.5 trillion. This sudden shift was especially unsettling because it came at the expense of the bottom 90 percent of the population. Particularly hard-hit, according to Wolff, were the poorest 40 percent of Americans—more than 100 million people—who suffered "an absolute decline in their average wealth holdings." They lost about $300 billion in assets, which meant their already meager net worth was rapidly approaching zero.[12]

The richest 1 percent of Americans pigged out throughout the 1980s, accumulating 61.6 percent of all wealth created in that period.[13] After a deep recession followed by very slow growth from 1989 to 1995, the U.S. economy began to grow again, but at a modest rate. Wealth was once again created

in ways that benefited the rich, most spectacularly in the huge run-up in stock prices between the middle of 1994 and the middle of 1997. Since the richest 1 percent of Americans owned nearly half of the stock,[14] they only had to sit back and watch the market. The overall value of publicly traded stocks increased from approximately $3 trillion in 1988 to $5 trillion in 1992 to well over $10 trillion in 1997.

One way to exemplify the astounding multiplication of the biggest fortunes is to look at the annual incomes they can generate. Andrew Hacker, in his book *Money: Who Has How Much and Why*, examined the people who reported incomes of over $1 million per year to the IRS. Their number, even after adjusting for inflation, had increased dramatically in fifteen years, from 13,505 in 1979 to 68,064 in 1994.[15]

The degree of inequality in the United States is now so extreme that we have returned to the ignominious levels of the 1920s.

PERCENTAGE OF WEALTH (TOTAL NET WORTH) HELD BY THE TOP 1% OF AMERICANS[16]					
1929	1949	1969	1979	1989	1995
44.2%	27.1%	31.1%	20.5%	35.7%	40%

No president, not even the loquacious Bill Clinton, could turn such economic statistics into a rosy prediction of good times ahead for the American people. The United States prospered most in those decades when circumstances and political forces caused the rich to share some of their fortunes and profits with the majority. But when the interests of the wealthy are placed *above* those of working Americans, as is true today, real prosperity becomes a distant dream.

1. Edward N. Wolff, *Top Heavy: A Study of the Increasing Inequality of Wealth in America*, New York: The New Press, 1996, and "Trends in Household Wealth in the United States During the 1980s," *Review of Income and Wealth*, June 1994, series 40, no. 2, Table 4. Wolff's rigorous studies are based in part on the Surveys of Consumer Finances (SCFs) conducted by the Federal Reserve Board; these, combined with a number of other studies on private fortunes, estate taxes, and inheritances, yield more accurate information than census data. The financial assets compared here come from the analysis of 1992 Federal Reserve statistics made by Wolff *(Top Heavy)* and by James M. Poterba and Andrew A. Samnick ("Stock Ownership Patterns, Stock Market Fluctuations, and Consumption," *Brookings Papers on Economic Activity*, Volume 2, 1995). The 1992 figures are the most recent available as of 1997; most likely they are conservative (that is, showing a smaller share for the very rich) compared with the actual share of financial assets owned in 1997, since the holdings of the rich ought to have been inflated the most by the stock market boom of the mid-1990s. See endnotes 5 and 13.

2. Lawrence Mishel, Jared Bernstein, and John Schmitt, *The State of Working America, 1996–97*, Armonk, NY: M. E. Sharpe, 1997, p. 149. In 1995, $7.28-per-hour full-time work was necessary to keep a family of four above the very low federal poverty threshhold. That year, 29.7 percent were at or below that wage, up from 23.7 percent in 1979.

3. Ravi Batra, *The Great American Deception*, p. 101.

4. Figures taken from tables 8.2 and 8.4 (and averaged), Mishel, Bernstein, and Schmitt, *The State of Working America*, 1997, pp. 384–88.

5. Percentages of each group are based on Wolff, *Top Heavy*, p. 67; I have modified his categories slightly: he used top 1 percent, next 19 percent, and bottom 80 percent, whereas I use top 1 percent, next 9 percent, and bottom 90 percent; in doing so I am relying on Wolff's more detailed categories in "Trends in Household Wealth in the United States, 1962–1983 and 1983–1989" (1994), and on Poterba and Samnick, "Stock Ownership Patterns, Stock Market Fluctuations, and Consumption" (1995).

I label the "affluent" as the "next 9 percent" that come after the "very rich," because I think this more accurately depicts the number of upper-middle class Americans who are not truly rich themselves but nevertheless have benefited from the growing disparities of income and wealth. See note 9 in chapter two for more discussion.

The figures for the average household wealth in dollars are my own, using the percentages of Wolff, Poterba, and Samnick and applying them to the U.S. economy in 1997 and conservatively reflecting some growth in the stock market and other economic assets. Although the dollar amounts are approximations, they accurately show the immense wealth disparities between each group.

6. Ibid., p. 64.

7. Maurice Zeitlin, "Who Owns America," *The Progressive*, June 1978, p. 5.

8. Lester Thurow quoted in Andrew Winnick, *Toward Two Societies: The Changing Distribution of Income and Wealth in the U.S. Since 1960*, New York: Praeger, 1989, pp. 184–85.

9. G. William Domhoff, *Who Rules America Now?*, Englewood Cliffs, NJ: Prentice Hall, 1983.

10. Wolff, "Trends in Household Wealth in the United States During the 1980s," *Review of Income and Wealth*, June 1994, series 40, no. 2, p. 171.

11. Ibid., p. 153. In 1989 the share of financial wealth held by the very rich is 48.3 percent, as opposed to the slightly lower figure for 1992, 46 percent. The 1992 number was generated at the end of an economic downturn when some sources of wealth—real estate values, business assets, interest-bearing accounts—declined in value temporarily. The stock market boom of the mid-1990s pushed the financial assets of the rich back up; by 1997 it would be safe to assume that those assets were equal to or greater than the 48.3 percent share the wealthy held in 1989. In any case, the lower 1992 figure is quite sufficient to demonstrate the overwhelming inequality that exists in the United States.

12. Ibid.

13. Mishel and Bernstein, *The State of Working America*, 1994, p. 248.

14. Poterba and Samnick, "Stock Ownership Patterns," p. 326.

15. Andrew Hacker, *Money: Who Has How Much and Why*, New York: Scribner, 1997, p. 73.

16. Wolff, 1996, pp. 78–96 and Ravi Batra, *The Great American Deception*, p. 172.

2

THE SINKING MAJORITY

 espite our pretensions to being a "middle-class" society, working people in the United States have seen their share of all personal income decline sharply over the past three decades. The 90 percent of the population at the bottom of the income scale, which used to collect 69 percent of the income, now collects only 59 percent. This means 10 percent of all personal income was redistributed upward, and most ended up in the hands of the richest 1 percent of all households.

SHARES OF INCOME COLLECTED BY AMERICAN HOUSEHOLDS[1]		
	1962	1992
The Very Rich (1% of the population)	9.3%	15.7%
The Affluent (the Next 9%)	21.5%	25.2%
The Rest of Us (90% of Americans)	69.2%	59.1%

How did the rich manage to get even richer? We know, having watched *Lifestyles of the Rich and Famous*, that the wealthy are not misers who put every penny they earn into their piggy banks. One reason the rich have been hogging the wealth is that they keep finding ways to earn more while the rest of us earn less.

From 1977 to 1994, real salaries and wages declined steadily for most people. For the 73 million Americans who work as private-sector employees—their ranks would include such people as nurses, truckers, office workers, retail clerks, machinists, construction workers, computer programmers, waiters, and miners—the average hourly pay fell by 13.1 percent.[2]

This steady downward trend was an unexpected blow to American families who had grown up in an age of prosperity. For thirty-two years after World War II, the median family income grew very handsomely, increasing by 111 percent between 1947 and 1979. Since then the median income has remained stagnant, rising ever so slightly from 1979 to 1989, then sinking 3.4 percent between 1989 and 1995.

MEDIAN FAMILY INCOME (IN INFLATION-ADJUSTED DOLLARS)[3]				
1947	1967	1979	1989	1995
$19,088	$33,305	$40,339	$42,049	$40,611

The only reason the median family income did not fall precipitously in the 1980s and early 1990s was that more people in each household, and women in particular, went to work. By 1996 women comprised almost half, or 46 percent, of the labor force. This increased the percentage of working-age people who were active in the labor force from 61.2 percent in 1975 to 67.3 percent in 1997. As a result of this trend, the overall number of hours worked per capita increased by 12 percent.

By the mid-1990s this intensive work effort had more or less stabilized, yet average families and single workers had little or nothing to show for all their effort. No matter how much they worked, people entering the labor force had trouble saving because they were earning much less than an equivalent worker would have earned a generation earlier. This was especially true for high school graduates with one to five years of work experience. In 1993 young men in this category were earning 30 percent less than their counterparts did in 1973, young women about 20 percent less. Young people with more education fared better, but not much. Even college graduates with one to five years of work experience had to settle for less; men's and women's wages were 8.5

percent and 7.3 percent respectively below those of comparable grads in 1973.[4]

The situation was also getting worse for more established households, such as married couples with children. At the median level for this group, family income grew from $46,476 in 1979 to $48,093 in 1994. In order to achieve this meager 3.5 percent increase in the face of declining wages, these husbands and wives had to work 17 percent more hours in 1994 than they did in 1979.

The Downward Pressure on the Working Class

When Americans refer to the "middle class" they are generally referring to middle-income people who might be more accurately described as "the decently paid portion of the working class." Most of us (90 percent of the population) are wage-earning people who do not have an independent profession or small business (much less a private fortune) and are dependent on steady wages and salaries for our survival and the well-being of our families. The overall downward trends in income affected most wage earners, not just those at the very bottom:

HOURLY WAGES OF MIDDLE-INCOME WORKERS[5]				
	1979	1989	1994	
30th Percentile	$ 8.11	$ 7.50	$ 7.22	down 11%
50th Percentile	$10.70	$10.30	$ 9.98	down 7%
70th Percentile	$14.56	$14.19	$14.00	down 4%

(The 30th percentile represents the level at which 30% of the population earned less and 70% earned more; the 70th percentile is the level at which 70% earned less and only 30% earned more.)

These wages were modest even in 1979, producing incomes between $15,000 and $30,000 per year. Most families needed two full-time wage-earners working harder than ever if they were going to be close to the median income of $40,611 in 1995. Some didn't have a chance: the wages of the lowest income men fell from $6.80 to $5.49 at the tenth percentile, and from $8.73 to $6.93 at the twentieth percentile; the situation for women was worse, for their wages fell to $4.84 from $5.82 at the tenth percentile and to $5.77 from $6.31 at the twentieth percentile. Male workers were losing the most ground: 18 percent at the twentieth percentile, 12 percent at the sixtieth, and 5 percent at the eightieth (women made some modest gains as gender bias diminished somewhat and new job categories opened up). Even at the high end, at the ninetieth percentile of all workers, where men earned almost $25 per hour, earnings did not go up at all.[6]

What's happening? Are we in the middle of an old-fashioned economic depression?

Not really, but there is ample reason for working people to be confused, discouraged, and, well . . . depressed. Wages have been falling even though labor productivity continues to rise and the workforce is much better educated than it was in the past. Average years of school completed by workers increased from 9.8 years in 1948 to 13.4 years in 1994. Cumulative productivity gains—the growth in the average amount of economic production per hour of work—totaled 25 percent from 1973 to 1995.[7] Since more Americans are now contributing more hours of labor than ever before, hours of work per capita have risen 12 percent in the last thirty years. If American incomes were really linked to the productivity of workers and the extra amount of work time expended—or to any possible combination of skill, education, and effort—median family incomes should have gone up 30 to 35 percent, rather than staying absolutely flat.

Sorting Out the Winners

In fact, overall income did keep growing in the United States over the past two decades— the average family income increased by 12 percent from 1979 to 1994—but all of the gains went to the top 20 percent of families. This was in stark contrast to the three previous decades, 1947 through 1979, when different segments of the population shared equally in exceptional income gains.

CHANGES IN FAMILY INCOMES[8]				
	1947–79	GAIN OR LOSS PER YEAR	1979–94	GAIN OR LOSS PER YEAR
Bottom Fifth:	+138%	+4.3%	−12%	−0.8%
Second Fifth:	+98%	+3.1%	−10%	−0.7%
Middle Fifth:	+106%	+3.3%	−4%	−0.3%
Fourth Fifth:	+114%	+3.6%	+4%	+0.3%
Top Fifth:	+99%	+3.1%	+31%	+2.1%

It would be misleading, however, to say that most people in the top 20 percent of the population were the big winners in the recent period from 1979 to 1994. After all, the top 20 percent is a very large number of people, over 50 million. More detailed analysis of this group suggests that only the top 1 percent made inordinate gains, while the rest received more reasonable increases in their incomes:

INCREASES IN INCOME AMONG THE TOP 20% OF AMERICAN FAMILIES[9]				
	1979	1994	% GAIN	GAIN PER YEAR
81st to 90th Percentiles	$72,210	$79,386	10%	+0.7%
91st to 99th Percentiles	$112,476	$141,433	26%	+1.7%
top 1%	$279,122	$560,090	101%	+6.7%

The gains made by the families between the 81st and 90th percentiles did not quite meet the modest level of overall growth in incomes (12 percent) generated by the American economy, while those in the next 9 percent (91st to 99th percentiles) did better than the average. Only the truly rich, the top 1 percent, made out like bandits. In fact, according to Edward N. Wolff, who calculates the unreported income of the rich more carefully than most other economists, the top 1 percent of households earned considerably more than the amount listed above, which is derived from U.S. census data that regularly understate the amount of property income collected. "In some years," writes Wolff, "reported property income is less than half of what national income and product accounts indicate it should be."[10]

Probably only the tax lawyers and accountants know for sure how much income has increased for the very wealthiest individuals. And the job of those accountants is to make pre-tax income look as low as possible. For example, while Wolff calculated that the average income of the top 1 percent was $672,000 in 1992, the average tax return for that group filed with the IRS in 1992 showed reported earnings of only $464,800.[11]

If we assume that the very rich took in roughly the same share of personal income in 1997 as they did in 1992 (a safe bet given the huge gains that were made in the stock market), then their average income was more than $800,000. The following figures illustrate the striking disparities that now exist among the three main income groups:

AVERAGE ANNUAL EARNINGS PER HOUSEHOLD, 1997[12]	
The Very Rich (the top 1%)	$825,000
The Affluent (the next 9%)	$150,000
The Rest of Us (the bottom 90%)	$35,000

Where Does It Come From?

Did the richest Americans, a little over a million households, really steal income away from the rest of the country?

Not exactly. But most of them certainly did not earn it by the sweat of their brows. Instead, they made money on their capital investments. The 1994 tax returns of 68,064 Americans showed incomes of more than $1 million. They also revealed the following: their ownership of stocks and bonds, other dividend and interest-producing investments, and sale of capital assets provided 38 percent of the income of such people; another 29 percent came via payouts from partnerships and personally held businesses; and finally, 33 percent came from salaries generated by business or professional employment.[13] Employment of the very rich can mean different things to different people; a few are the highest paid corporate CEOs and a small number are highly paid entertainers, including sports stars. However, many other wealthy people draw salaries from businesses they own, even if they don't contribute their labor.

When we note that the incomes of the wealthiest have increased so much faster than those of the rest of the population, it is futile to look for the explanation in changes in the structure of jobs, or in the increased education levels of a particular part of the population. It is not accurate to blame the inadequacies of the American family, as do some apologists for the status quo, for dragging the majority of the population down; nor is there much evidence that those few at the top have achieved their gains by playing according to the rules of a meritocracy. (For a brief discussion of some factors that do not really affect falling or rising salaries very much, please see note 14.)[14]

In effect, wealthy Americans have been appropriating part of the national income, about 10 percent, that used to go to other citizens. And their gain has been spectacular indeed: about $700 billion a year in income that once went to others in the form of higher wages for their labor is now being transferred to the very rich each year.

In the 1990s, there were at least two kinds of big gainers. The most noticeable were the tiny minority made up of the corporate CEOs who run American business. In 1995 they delivered the goods to their corporations—the highest rates of profit ever—and they reaped the benefits. *Business Week* announced in the spring of 1996: "CEO Pay Up 30% at the Fortune 500 Corporations in 1995. Total compensation averages $3,746,392."[15]

In part these men at the top were being rewarded for their efforts to drive down the wages of ordinary Americans. (See chapter 8.) The consequences of such efforts were dramatic. By 1995 the average American factory worker only earned 67 percent of the median family income, far below the 89 percent average of 1955. The worker in retail sales fared even worse, dropping from 57 percent of median family earnings to just 29 percent over forty years. Add the two together and the results are sobering. A working class couple in 1955, one laboring full-time in manufacturing and the other in retail, could do very well. Their combined pay averaged well above—about 146 percent—the median family income. In 1995 the situation was grim: two full-time

workers in these same occupations could not even make it to the median.[16]

If the income generated by our growing economy was not rewarding labor, then it had to be multiplying the holdings of capital. The largest income gains in this category, less visible than CEO salaries, were enjoyed by the majority of the rich. Their earnings have almost no relation to their work but directly correlate with their economic assets. In 1996 some of the long-term major stockholders in America's corporations were choosing to cash in on their huge successes in the stock market. Charles Dorrance, who had inherited his wealth through the Campbell soup family, traded in 9 million shares of company stock on Halloween of 1996 and "earned" a treat of $740 million.

Other capitalists sat back and enjoyed the thought of unprecedented, yet-to-be-realized capital gains. For Warren Buffet, the renowned investor, the stock ticker noted that another $10.6 billion was added to his fortune over a period of twenty-four months; his total wealth doubled to $21 billion.[17] He was a beneficiary of the largesse produced by our giant political economy, and his good fortune illustrates why the United States has returned to a level of inequality not seen since 1929. All the gains won by the working classes in the middle of the twentieth century, and sustained through the 1950s, 1960s, and 1970s, have been lost. Is it possible that the 1990s will end up even more unfair than the 1920s?

1. From Edward N. Wolff, *Top Heavy*, 1996, p. 67, and James M. Poterba and Andrew A. Samnick, "Stock Ownership Patterns, Stock Market Fluctuations, and Consumption," *Brookings Papers on Economic Activity*, Volume 2, 1995, p. 326; both are based on analysis of *Surveys of the Financial Characteristics of Consumers* (*SCFs*), published by the Federal Reserve Board for 1962 and 1992.

Census data corroborate the same trend, showing that an 8.2 percent share of all personal income was redistributed upward, from the bottom 80 percent to the top 20 percent.

SHARES OF INCOME COLLECTED BY AMERICAN HOUSEHOLDS		
	THE TOP 20%	THE BOTTOM 80%
1968	40.5%	59.5%
1994	48.7%	51.3%

The only problem with census data is that they do not adequately measure the income of the very rich, thus underestimating the shares of income received by the top 1 percent and the top 10 percent. Wolff's sophisticated methodology for tracking the rich is unmatched, thus the reliance on 1992 data to show the long-term pattern of transfer of income from the majority to the very top. There is no indication in the late 1990s that this trend could have been reversed (although it is possible, given the level of speculative wealth that is being traded, that the share of the rich may have grown even larger). For more discussion, see endnote 9 of this chapter.

2. Ravi Batra, *The Great American Deception*, p. 9.

3. Mishel, Bernstein, and Schmitt, "The State of American Workers," *Challenge*, November–December 1996, p. 41. The median refers to the family that is exactly halfway, at the 50th percentile, between the very top and the very bottom. Because all the overall income gains in the past twenty years have gone to the top, it is possible for the median to stay stagnant even though the average of all household incomes has increased by 12 percent.

4. Mishel, Bernstein, and Schmitt, 1997, p. 176.

5. Jared Bernstein, "Anxiety Over Wages Is Justified," *Challenge*, July–August 1996, p. 60. Since 1994 there has been no appreciable change in wages, according to the government statistics issued in *Economic Indicators*; this was in spite of the fact that the United States was in a period of cyclical economic upturn, a time when workers used to make substantial gains in earnings.

6. Mishel, Bernstein, and Schmitt, 1997, pp. 143–44.

7. Mishel, Bernstein, and Schmitt, *The State of Working America*, 1997, p. 33.

8. Campaign for America's Future, "Here We Go Again," *The Nation*, pp. 18–19, September 2, 1996. Numbers are based on analysis by Mishel, Bernstein, and Schmitt in *The State of Working America*, 1997.

9. Derived from Mishel, Bernstein, and Schmitt, *The State of Working America*, 1997, pp. 60–61. The reader will find no better data and analysis on income change and the reasons for falling wages and salaries than this study provides; the authors update the book every two years. Because their use of various census data and reports is more thoroughgoing than other analyses, I feel that it is generally better to rely on their 1994 numbers than to deal with partial information available through 1997.

For reasons of consistency with the wealth statistics, I have chosen to divide up the income statistics into the same categories: top 1 percent, next 9 percent, and bottom 90 percent. Many representations of the data show the top 20 percent as a group that has benefited at the expense of everyone else (census data most often appears in this format). But the common practice of representing income and wealth in quintiles (five groups of 20 percent each) can promote misconceptions. By lumping together the more than 50 million Americans in the top 20 percent, it appears that a huge portion of Americans are either outperforming the rest of us or taking great advantage of us. Although this is theoretically possible, it is not borne out by the statistics themselves.

For instance, the people in the 81st to 90th percentiles (the bottom half of the top quintile) don't fit into the higher group (top 10 percent), which gained at the expense of the rest of us in the last two decades. Even this second-highest 10 percent, made up of skilled, generally well-educated Americans (they have the highest proportion of dual worker households and total hours worked) only earns 15 percent of the national income; that is to say, one family in this group earns about 1.5 times as much as the average for all families. Most likely the workers in these families are contributing skills, extra labor time, or experience that others lack. Their percentage of all personal income has stayed almost exactly the same for the past thirty years, so this group has not been the beneficiary of the upward redistribution of income. As we might expect, its source of income is overwhelmingly from its labor, not from capital. The modest capital component of 9.6 percent is hardly different from other working people below them: 8 percent for both the fourth quintile (61st to 80th percentiles) and the third quintile (41st to 60th percentiles).

As for the affluent upper-middle class—the 9 percent below the top 1 percent—they did see their incomes increase by more than the average, but they were completely outpaced by the very rich. The very rich collected two and half times as much income (per household) as the affluent did in 1979, and four times as much in the early 1990s, and probably (by best current estimates) more than five times as much as of 1997.

10. Wolff, *Top Heavy*, 1996. In an endnote on page 90, Wolff discusses the problem of tracking the income of the rich: "Asset income is generally not well reported. Income statistics in the United States are generally based on census data. Although coverage of wage and salary income is quite good, these data typically substantially understate property income such as dividends, interest, and rent. In some years, reported property income is less than half of what the national income and product accounts indicate it should be."

11. Ibid., p. 68, and Donald L. Barlett and James B. Steele, *America: Who Stole the Dream?*, Kansas City: Andrews and McMeel, 1996, p. 6.

12. These are my approximations, which apply to the total personal income for 1997, and based on the proportions calculated by Wolff for 1992. Since in-depth analysis of incomes in the mid-to-late 1990s is not yet available, it is possible that my estimates are off by a few thousand dollars; however, the numbers should accurately portray the astounding disparities in incomes that separate the three groups. If anything they will underestimate the huge gains made by the richest citizens through the financial speculation that was rampant between 1993 and 1997.

13. Andrew Hacker, *Money*, p. 82.

14. The growing inequality in incomes in the 1980s has often been attributed to education differentials, suggesting that only those who had completed college would be able to enjoy higher incomes. This idea of meritocracy has been heartily endorsed, not only by wealthy conservatives who liked to justify their own good fortunes, but also by liberals. Robert Reich dubbed the high achievers "symbolic analysts," people trained to perform economically useful brainwork that other workers could not. This argument did not account for the downward trend in wages that began to affect college graduates, too. By 1993, all people with four years of college were earning 2 percent less than they had been six years earlier.

Another interpretation, quite popular with journalists and political pundits, is that inequality in family incomes must have been produced by the increasing number of well-paid women workers who are married to equally well-paid males. This is a clever, meritocratic argument that tries to shift some of the blame for inequality of income to the increase in gender equality in employment; the idea is that the best-educated of both sexes have been able to land all the best jobs, work very long hours, and marry each other. While anecdotal evidence from various workplaces suggests this might be true, it is not born out by economic analysis. In fact, by the 1990s the evidence pointed the other way: in families which had the top 5 percent of incomes from 1989 to 1994, the wives were actually decreasing their working hours substantially (unlike all other families) because their average family incomes, which had already soared in the 1980s, were soaring again (from $262,064 to $308,213 per year, according to Mishel, Bernstein, and Schmitt, *The State of Working America*, p. 83). There are, of course, many couples in our society in which both wives and husbands are high-earning professionals and managers; they are, however, statistically insignificant compared to other high-income households that do not need two earners anymore.

For a sophisticated analysis of these factors, and a debunking of a variety of other explanations of the deterioration of the American standard of living (and a point-by-point dismissal of the myth that most people are doing just fine) see "Introduction: the Living Standards Debate" in *The State of Working America*. It assigns a percentage of wage losses to the real culprits: institutional factors such as deunionization of the work force and a falling minimum wage, 33 percent; the growth of low-wage service employment compared to the decline in manufacturing jobs, 20 percent; the downward pressure from the globalization of trade and labor markets, 15–25 percent, etcetera. Various segments of David M. Gordon's *Fat and Mean* (NY: Free Press, 1996) provide similar analysis with a somewhat different emphasis.

15. "How High Can CEO Pay Go?," *Business Week*, April 22, 1996, p. 101.

16. Barlett and Steele, *America: Who Stole the Dream?*, p. 123.

17. *New York Times*, August 18, 1996, Business section, p. 2, and *Forbes*, October 1997.

3

WELL-TO-DO-FARE

Federal programs for the well-to-do, in the form of massive tax reductions, have helped the richest citizens acquire and maintain their wealth in the 1980s and 1990s. As the chart below demonstrates, we no longer have the system of progressive taxation that we had from the 1950s to the 1970s, when the U.S. economy was generally very strong.

The decline of most people's incomes and the increase in the fortunes of the rich did not occur without political assistance. Our governments—at the state, local, and federal levels—have helped facilitate the process for over twenty years. The process began in 1977 when Jimmy Carter and a Democratic Congress were kind enough to lower the capital gains tax.

During the 1980s the Reagan administration and the Congress were even more

MAXIMUM TAX RATES OF THE RICHEST AMERICANS[1]			
	1950s THROUGH THE 1970s	1980s	1990s
Federal Income Tax	70%–91%*	28%–50%	31%–39.6%
Capital Gains Tax	25%–49%	20%–28%	20%–28%
The Effective Rate of Tax on Corporate Profits[2]	36%–48%	22%–35%	26%–28%

*Each pair of numbers shows the range of tax rates assessed during each time period.

generous than their predecessors with well-to-do-fare for the rich. For instance, the federal "tax reform" bill of 1981 cut the income tax rates for all Americans in 1982, but the benefits were not equally distributed among all families. The tax bill, loudly advertised as offering relief to everyone, was designed to serve the wealthy.

EFFECTS OF "TAX REFORM" ON A FAMILY OF FOUR (IN 1982 DOLLARS)	
FAMILY INCOME	FEDERAL INCOME TAX SAVINGS
$20,000	$224
$50,000	$1,114
$100,000	$15,237

The general trend in federal legislation was to reverse the system of progressive taxation on corporations and the rich and to make working people shoulder the burden. The taxes on labor income (earned income)— in particular, the increased Social Security taxes on wages and salaries imposed under the Reagan administration in 1983—rose so that taxes on capital income (unearned investment income) could fall dramatically:

TAX RATES ON DIFFERENT KINDS OF INCOME		
	1966	1985
Labor Income	17.6%	20.6%
Capital Income	33%	17.5%[3]

The process was not over, for in 1986, more federal "tax reform" legislation furthered the trend by reducing the top income tax rate to 28 percent, its lowest level since the 1920s. The results of the law became evident in documents compiled by the Internal Revenue Service a few years later:

BENEFITS OF THE "TAX REFORM" ACT OF 1986[4]		
INCOME	PERCENTAGE CUT	TAX SAVINGS
$30,000–$40,000	11%	$467
$75,000–$100,000	18%	$3,034
$1,000,000 and Up	31%	$281,033

The overall effect of the changes in tax law, from the reduction in capital gains taxes that began in the late 1970s through the Reagan administration tax breaks for the rich in the 1980s, was to increase the after-tax incomes of the rich. While the pretax incomes of the top 1 percent increased 78 percent between 1977 and 1989, their after-tax incomes increased by an astounding 102 percent.[5]

During the Bush administration there was some tinkering with tax rates—the maximum tax rate moved up slightly, to 31 percent in 1991—but this did not reverse the above trends in the least. The rich, of course, have always employed various loopholes for avoiding taxation and generally pay their taxes at rates well below the official maximums. The experience of one prominent millionaire household, that of President George Bush and his wife, Barbara, illustrates how the real tax rate often fell much lower. For 1991, the Bush family reported an adjusted gross income of $1,324,456, paid a federal income tax of 14.7 percent, and ended up with a bargain rate of 18.1 percent for all federal, state, and local taxes combined. In the same year, a family with the median income of $35,939 paid 27.6 percent of their income in combined federal, state, and local taxes.[6]

The "Mansion Subsidy"

These blatant tax cuts are easy to identify, but it is also worth looking at an example of well-to-do-fare in disguise. The homeowner's deduction for mortgage interest is a popular piece of tax legislation that is supposed to help middle-income Americans own a home. During the early 1980s mortgage interest rates reached such high levels that many potential home buyers were simply excluded from the market; this was one of the factors that led to the first decrease in overall home ownership since

World War II. The well-to-do were not discouraged, however, from buying mansions and extra vacation houses. This was because the home owner's deduction was particularly beneficial for people in the highest tax brackets, and almost meaningless for the average citizen. For instance, in 1982, when mortgage rates were at 12 percent, the average family with a taxable income of $20,000 could buy an average house and, due to the effect of the tax deduction, have their interest rate effectively reduced to 10.7 percent. A family earning $100,000 and buying a high-priced house enjoyed the full measure of the tax deduction, which reduced their effective interest rate to an entirely painless 1.4 percent.[7]

By the late 1980s and 1990s, interest rates for mortgages had dropped considerably, but wealthy and near-wealthy homeowners were still the primary beneficiaries of mortgage interest deductions. In 1995 the federal government lost $51 billion in tax revenues because of the mortgage deduction, nearly twice the amount, $26 billion, spent on all low-income housing programs and rental subsidies by the Department of Housing and Urban Development. The Joint Taxation Committee of Congress showed that the richest 5 percent of Americans, those with incomes over $100,000 per year, collected 44 percent of the homeowner subsidy in 1995, for a total of $22.5 billion. Those earning over $200,000 per year were eager to cash in on their housing assistance; 71 percent of them used the mortgage deduction. Meanwhile, the large majority of poor Americans did not get any housing assistance from the government, for the mortgage deduction is virtually unusable for poor home owners and only 29 percent of the poor resided in public or other kinds of subsidized housing.[8]

Compounding Self-Interest

When well-to-do-fare is not granted directly through personal tax cuts and tax deductions, it is indirectly encouraged by the changes in laws affecting corporations and individually owned businesses. The taxes generated by corporate profits have fallen by almost half, from 3.3 percent of gross domestic product (GDP) in the 1960s to 1.9 percent in the 1990s. Over this period the tax rates were lowered; but more importantly a series of adjustments, loopholes, and tax credits helped cut the effective tax rate on corporate profits in half, from nearly 50 percent to between 22 and 28 percent. Some whopping giveaways, such as the one that awards over $10 billion to the major corporations that import oil, predated the declining rates and still exist.[9] The various exemptions and special treatment for corporate America—which include everything from hefty tobacco industry subsidies to incentives to sell more Big Macs in other parts of the world—have been criticized by conservatives and liberals alike. The libertarian, right-wing think tank, the Cato Institute, estimated that direct subsidies of "corporate welfare" added up to $86.2 billion per year in 1995.[10] The more centrist Progressive Policy Institute found that indefensible corporate tax breaks added up to $53 billion per year.[11]

Not all favoritism is granted through taxes—some of the most important services to the wealthy are provided by quasigovernment agencies. The most powerful and influential of these is the Federal Reserve Board, which regulates the nation's money supply with the primary purpose of looking after the well-being of the banking and finance industries. William Greider, in his book *Secrets of the Temple*, described how the Federal Reserve Board kept interest rates artificially high through most of the 1980s when it restricted the money supply in order to contain inflation.[12] The result was a "real interest rate" (the difference between the interest on federal funds and the rate of inflation) which averaged 4.8 percent, far above the rate of the previous three decades. This represented a staggering transfer of funds to the monied classes because ordinary working Americans had deflated incomes, caused by stagnant or falling wages, at the same time they were borrowing money (for such things as homes, cars, and appliances) at grossly inflated rates.[13]

In an earlier era, at the end of the nineteenth century, the banking trusts multiplied the fortunes of the Robber Barons by actively pursuing monetary deflation, a policy that drove down wages while automatically increasing the worth of the accumulating fortunes of the rich. In effect, the Federal Reserve Board performed a similar function in the 1980s by favoring "unearned" income over income generated by labor. In 1960 interest income equaled only 8.4 percent of wage and salary income; but when interest rates skyrocketed during the 1980s, personal income from interest rose, too, reaching $680 billion in 1990, an amount equal to 25.2 percent of all wage and salary income. Interest rates finally declined in the 1990s, but the percentage of interest income, which went mostly to those who had accumulated money during the previous decade, remained quite high; it equaled 21 percent of all wage and salary income in 1996.

With the modest interest rates and lower rates of inflation that have characterized the 1990s, income from bank deposits became less popular with the well-to-do. They, as well as many middle-class citizens who had some savings, began transferring cash into the stock market and watching their speculative earnings rise at a phenomenal rate. When the U.S. economy finally showed signs of growing at respectable rates in 1996 and 1997, one might have thought that it was time for working people to finally make up for the steady losses in earning power they had suffered in the two previous decades. Not so. For whenever the government's quarterly wage reports indicated that earnings might creep ahead of the inflation rate, the chairman of the Federal Reserve, Allan Greenspan—backed by a chorus of voices from the corporations, banks, and business media—immediately suggested that the Federal Reserve might have to raise interest rates again to slow down the economy. While these comments were designed to help corporations keep a tight lid on labor costs, the Federal Reserve did not have a plan for restraining the more real threat to our economy posed by the excesses of capital. In fact, after his remark about "unwarranted exuberance" made the financial markets shudder in late 1996, Chairman Greenspan decided he should act bullish about the future of the stock market.

Did Greenspan really think the boom in financial securities could go on forever? Or was he just crossing his fingers and praying that the speculative binge on Wall Street, fueled by years of generous handouts from our well-to-do-fare system, would end in a mild "correction" instead of a crash?

1. Donald L. Barlett and James B. Steele, *America: Who Really Pays the Taxes?*, New York: Simon & Schuster, 1994. Ravi Batra, *The Great American Deception*, p. 60.

2. Mishel, Bernstein, and Schmitt, *The State of Working America 1997*, p. 124. One of the reasons that the effective rate of taxation has fallen is that corporations have been able to move large portions of their profits into untaxed categories.

3. Joseph Pechman, *Who Paid the Taxes, 1966–1985?*, Washington, D.C.: Brookings Institute, 1985.

4. The IRS data for 1989 tax returns (which were governed by the 1986 tax law) reported in the *Philadelphia Inquirer*, October 21, 1991.

5. Mishel and Bernstein, *The State of Working America*, Armonk, N.Y.: M. E. Sharpe, 1994, p. 89 (an earlier edition of the work cited above).

6. Barlett and Steele, pp. 17–18.

7. Steve Brouwer, "Mortgage deductions are bonanzas—for the rich," *Ithaca Journal*, March 3, 1983, p. 12. The calculations are based on assumptions, appropriate for that year and that housing market, that the average family earning $20,000 could afford a house with a $25,000 mortgage, and that a wealthy family earning $100,000 could afford a $200,000 mortgage.

8. All the figures in this paragraph come from national housing experts Peter Dreier and John Atlas, "Mansions on the Hill," *In These Times*, June 26, 1995, pp. 22–23. The "mansion subsidy" not only favors the richest owners, it also promotes the construction of the most lavish houses. The owner with a $1.25 million house and a $1 million mortgage enjoyed a tax deduction of approximately $380,000, according to one congressional report in 1995. When legislators recommended limiting the housing deduction to "only" the first $300,000 of mortgage money borrowed, the housing and banking industries successfully battled to keep the whole deduction.

9. See Barlett and Steele, pp. 183–89, for a description of the Saudi Arabian oil scam, in which royalties paid were transformed into foreign taxes. This has entitled the major oil companies to drastically lower their U.S. taxes ever since the early 1950s, by an amount said to exceed $10 billion per year.

10. Robert D. Hershey, Jr., "A Hard Look at Corporate Welfare," *New York Times*, March 7, 1995, p. D1.

11. Ibid.

12. William Greider, *Secrets of the Temple: How the Federal Reserve Runs the Country*, New York: Simon & Schuster, 1987.

13. Over the previous three decades (1948–79), the real interest rate had been very low, fluctuating from −.3 percent to 1.7 percent; since average workers and their families were making substantial gains in income in those years, they were able to erase some of the advantages held by the very rich. They borrowed at very low interest and accumulated some property, thus making the distribution of wealth more equal. Real interest rates come from Samuel Bowles, David M. Gordon, and Thomas E. Weisskopf, *Beyond the Wasteland: A Democratic Economics for the Year 2000*, Armonk, NY: M. E. Sharpe, 1990, p. 124.

4

HAVE TAXES BEEN KILLING THE UNITED STATES?

eath and taxes are said to be inevitable, but this does not mean that taxation is deadly. Overall tax rates, as a percentage of what our economy produces, have been remarkably stable over the past three decades. Furthermore, our total taxation of both individuals and corporations has stayed at a moderate level, well below that of all of the advanced Western European countries and about the same as that of the frugal Japanese.[1]

The fact that rich Americans are convinced that their taxes are killing them should not surprise us. Nor should the fact that the politically vocal among their ranks—New Jersey governor Christine Todd Whitman, George Bush and his son, the governor of Texas, not to mention multimillionaires Steve Forbes and Ross Perot—are intent on lowering taxes and keeping them low.

Unfortunately, many other Americans also think that taxes have risen too high in recent decades; and, because they have been misled about the overall situation, they often vote for politicians who cater to the rich. Average citizens do not generally benefit from the kinds of tax reductions that follow, but they are correct in believing that taxation is an increasing burden for them.

We have a complicated mix of personal taxes at various governmental levels. Most state and local taxes fall heavily on lower-

U.S. TAX REVENUE AS A PERCENTAGE OF GROSS DOMESTIC PRODUCT[2]		
	FEDERAL	STATE AND LOCAL	TOTAL
1973	19.1%	10.5%	29.6%
1979	20.0%	9.8%	29.8%
1989	19.8%	10.3%	30.1%
1996	19.9%	10.8%	30.7%

income groups, while federal income tax is one of the few ways of collecting taxes on high-income people.

PERCENTAGE OF INCOME THAT GOES TO DIFFERENT TAXES, AS COLLECTED FROM VARIOUS INCOME GROUPS IN 1996[3]

AVERAGE INCOME OF DIFFERENT HOUSEHOLDS	FEDERAL INCOME TAX	SOCIAL SECURITY AND MEDICARE	STATE, LOCAL, AND FEDERAL EXCISE	TOTAL TAXATION RATE
Bottom 20% ($8,413)	−6.9%*	7.7%	16.8%	17.6%
Middle 20% ($34,501)	6.1%	10.2%	10.9%	27.2%
Top 20% ($93,456)†	12.9%	9.7%	8.3%	30.9%
Top 1% ($632,330)	24.4%	3.1%	6.3%	33.8%

*The negative tax represents the earned income credit of poor workers.
†Not including the top 1%.

When we add all these numbers together we find that the middle-income household, at $34,501, was paying almost as high a percentage of its income toward taxes, 27.2 percent, as the very rich household, which paid 33.5 percent. Even our poor, who are very poor indeed, paid at a substantial rate. Thus, even though our income taxes have a progressive component, the regressive taxes nearly balance them out in the overall tax rates.

This is something new. While figures show that the proportion of economic output that society as a whole devotes to paying taxes has scarcely changed at all (U.S. Tax Revenue as a Percentage of Gross Domestic Product, listed on the previous page), the burden of taxation on different segments of American society has changed. Those with sharp eyes will notice that total taxes as a percentage of GDP have gone up by about a single percentage point in the past three decades. Yet federal income taxes on all households stayed the same, 11.1 percent of GDP in the 1970s and 11.2 percent in the

1990s, while corporate income taxes were cut almost in half, from 3.3 percent of GDP to 1.9 percent.[4] The one component of taxation that rose significantly was the federal payroll tax, which accounted for 8.9 percent of GDP in 1996 as opposed to 6.5 percent in 1977.

For most of the period between 1977 and 1996, and especially following the passage of Social Security tax laws during the Reagan administration (1983), increasing Social Security and Medicare (FICA) rates were levied on ever-greater amounts of the income of working and middle-class citizens. This brought in much more revenue than was necessary to pay out Social Security benefits to retired and disabled citizens; the money was applied to other areas of the federal budget to make up, but only in part, for the budget deficit and for the shortfall in collecting taxes from the rich.[5]

The rising payroll taxes, along with the growing burden of income taxes on households near the median, helped increase inequality by leveling the tax rates of people from different classes. Taking the long view, back to the 1950s, we see the huge impact of the steady shift away from progressive taxation: in the mid-1950s, the working-class family with the median income paid a federal tax rate (income tax and Social Security combined) of 9 percent; in the mid-1990s it was paying 16.7 percent. On the other hand, the super-rich person earning over $1 million in the mid-1950s paid an effective federal income tax rate of 85.5 percent; in the mid-1990s, when there were a lot more million-dollar earners, this tax rate had plunged to 32 percent.[6]

Changes in taxation did not create the increasing inequality in the United States, but it certainly exacerbated it. In no uncertain terms, we changed from a nation where everyone's incomes grew rapidly and at an equal pace (from the 1950s to the 1970s, as outlined in the previous chapter) to one where most people's incomes stagnated or fell, while only the richest made spectacular gains (from the 1970s to the 1990s). Thus, it was only adding insult to injury to require the large majority of Americans—the lower and middle classes—to bear a larger share of the tax load over the past twenty years.

Capital Guys Prefer Capital Gains

By the beginning of the 1990s, the rich were probably thinking that the more intricate forms of well-to-do-fare were no longer necessary as methods of avoiding taxation. The dream of Andrew Mellon and many wealthy old conservatives of the 1920s had been answered.[7] The federal income tax, intended to progressively tax the rich ever since it was instituted in 1913, was no longer graduated enough to achieve progressive results. And who knows if the wealthiest Americans were even paying these taxes? If the rich, or their tax lawyers, were cheating on their tax returns, the Internal Revenue Service did not have the funding or the manpower to catch them. The *Wall Street Journal* reported on April 15, 1991, that the IRS was concentrating its audits on the middle class because the tax returns of the rich and the corporations were too complicated and too easily contested in court.

Just as wealthy taxpayers were getting comfortable with the inevitability of low taxes, they were shocked in 1993 when the newly elected President, Bill Clinton, and his Democratic Congress dared to raise the top federal income tax rates a little, though not nearly enough to approach the rates that had been maintained from the 1930s through the 1970s. The official maximum tax was fixed at 39.6 percent for income over $256,500 in 1995, and the effective rate of federal income tax on the wealthiest 1 percent of Americans (what was actually collected) inched back up to 24.9 percent.[8] The Clinton administration's tax increase enraged many upper-class and upper-middle-class people, even though it did little to close the gap between the wealthy and the rest of American society.

For one thing, the Clinton tax bill of 1993 did not dare touch the maximum capital gains tax, which remained at 28 percent. Capital gains are the profits made, or "realized," from the sales of stocks, real estate, and other financial assets. Since the rich own such a huge proportion of the nation's wealth, especially its financial and business assets, they gain or lose disproportionately when the capital gains taxes are modified.[9] According to the business section of the *New York Times* in 1989, approximately 60 percent of capital gains were raked in by only $2/_{10}$ths of 1 percent of the people, and 80 percent by the top 1 percent.[10] Throughout the whole process of implementing well-to-do-fare, there was steady attention paid to the tax on realized capital gains: they were lower in the 1980s and 1990s—ranging between 20 and 28 percent—than in earlier decades.

This great windfall merely whetted the appetite of the well-to-do. George Bush tried to lower the tax to 15 percent in 1991 and Robert Dole, running for president in 1996, offered to lower the capital gains rate to 14 percent. Steve Forbes, the multimillionaire who pushed a flat tax during his campaign for the Republican nomination in 1996, wanted to do away with the capital gains tax altogether.

Although the Republicans did not win the presidency in 1996, the rich had succeeded in rallying the Congress and the Democratic administration to their cause. They quickly succeeded in rolling back their taxes again. In the hodgepodge of tax legislation that Clinton and the Republican Congress cobbled together in the summer of 1997, the big winners were those who wanted a lower capital gains tax; it was reduced immediately to 20 percent, and was set at 18 percent for the year 2001. For good measure, the President and the Congress also agreed to cut inheritance taxes on wealthy Americans. Preliminary analysis of the new tax law—including such items as credits for college tuition and children, as well as the capital gains-cut—indicated that half of the benefits would go to the top 5 percent of the population.[11]

Supply-Side Revival

One of the congressmen who led the call for these tax reductions was Dick Armey, the House majority leader. During the conservative Republican resurgence in Congress between 1994 and 1996, he had dedicated much of his time to counterattacking Clinton's halfhearted efforts at progressive taxation in 1993. His program, outlined in his book, *The Flat Tax*, became the foundation of the campaigns of the serious Republican presidential contenders, Bob Dole and Steve Forbes; it also pushed the Clinton administration much further to the right. While a few of Armey's ideas for simplifying the tax code were admirable, such as getting rid of mortgage deductions, he had clearly designed a "flat" income tax to benefit the wealthy. Although the rich seemed to lose by giving up various deductions, they gained much more from his lower, universal tax rate. Two professors of accounting at DePaul University, David Roberts and Mark Sullivan, appraised the plan this way: "If the wealthiest individuals in America were to get together with the

goal of designing a tax that would most benefit them, they would have a hard time coming up with something better than a flat tax."[12]

But Armey's flat income tax was not really flat; it was regressive. It was a device to allow the rich to pay at a lower rate than everyone else. Economist Robert Eisner demonstrated that Armey's tax would have a very difficult time producing enough revenue for the government, and, more important, that taxes would increase slightly for almost everyone with incomes below $200,000 while those with incomes above $200,000 would see their federal income tax rates cut in half, to 12.7 percent.[13]

Armey's goal was to launch a revival of the "supply-side" economics that had characterized the Reagan administration. While the "flat tax" itself faded away after the 1996 election, the political climate had been altered in favor of tax reductions for the rich, in particular the capital gains measures so enthusiastically promoted by the Clinton administration in 1997. Both political parties seemed to be buying into some version of supply-side ideas, which argued that by increasing the income available to the rich, the government would set off a boom in productive investment. In Dick Armey's words: "There's more money available for investment and savings. . . . More things are produced and created. When that happens, wages go up and the general standard of living rises."[14]

This never happened the first time the scenario was played out, between 1980 and 1990, when the Reagan and Bush administrations used the same rationale for their tax policies. Most people's incomes fell and never recovered, demonstrating that huge tax cuts do not create high-paying jobs. The tightfisted, virtuous capitalists—whom sociologist Max Weber once admired for their Protestant ethic, their personal austerity, and their dedication to long-term investment—were seldom to be found. Even though the rich and the near-rich increased their incomes, the nation's overall rate of personal savings fell by about half, to under 5 percent.[15] Our society invested extraordinary sums of money in these people and received no return at all. The wealthy had nearly devoured the whole pie.

The fact that low tax rates were still prescribed as the remedy for our economic ills at the end of the 1990s demonstrated only one thing: that the well-to-do exercised a great deal of power and influence over politics. And to divert attention from their dominance, they concentrated their energy on demonizing and chastising the poor.

1. The Organization for Economic Cooperation and Development (OECD) reported in 1995 on the 1993 tax rates of all Western European countries, Japan, Australia, New Zealand, and Canada. All had overall tax rates that were between 35 percent and 53 percent (as percentage of GDP), except for Japan and Australia, which were at 29.1 percent and 28.7 percent, respectively.

2. Mishel, Bernstein, and Schmitt, *The State of Working America 1997*, p. 102.

3. Ibid., pp. 116, 127, based on Congressional Budget Office figures.

4. Ibid., p. 124.

5. See Barlett and Steele, *America: Who Really Pays the Taxes?* pp. 105–10, for more details. By 1993 the payroll contributions for Social Security and Medicare, 40.8 percent of the money collected at the federal level, had surpassed the total brought in by all individual income taxes, 39.9 percent. The contrast with the 1960s is stark: income taxes then provided more of federal revenues, 42 percent, and payroll taxes contributed only 18.4 percent. To a large degree, the extra Social Security revenues in the 1980s and 1990s were offsetting the steep decline in corporate income taxes, down to 11.3 percent of federal revenue as opposed to 20.4 percent throughout the 1960s.

6. Kevin Phillips, *Boiling Point*, New York: Random House, 1993, p. 107; Andrew Hacker, *Money*, p. 83.

7. See Barlett and Steele, pp. 64–67, for a description of Andrew Mellon's single-minded devotion to reducing the taxes of millionaires like himself during the period from World War I to the Great Depression.

8. Joseph Pechman, at the time the nation's premier tax researcher at the Brookings Institute, estimated that the effective tax rate on the rich household in 1985 was either the same as or lower than the total taxes collected from the median-income household.

9. Although after-tax incomes increased as a result of reduced taxes on realized capital gains (that is, on items actually sold), there is a larger, more subtle benefit to the preference for capital gains. Economist Robert Shapiro concluded that this was a major factor contributing to the increasing disparity in wealth and incomes in the 1980s: "The top 1 percent own vast capital assets, the value of which increased when tax incentives artificially raised their rate of return." That is, when certain kinds of investments are given strong tax preference (whether it be in capital gains or something else), money from investors pours in, as into the stock market in the 1990s; the excitement and pressure from this shift of investment causes these asset values to rise faster than they normally would, thus rewarding the investors with higher returns even before they sell their assets and pay a lower capital gains tax. Shapiro, "Invest," *The New Republic*, December 23, 1991, p. 17.

10. David E. Rosenbaum, "Capital Gains: Politics and Poor Data," *New York Times*, Business Section, October 1, 1989, p. 1.

11. From the tax watchdog group Citizens for Tax Justice, *The Nation*, August 25–September 1, 1997, p. 4.

12. David Roberts and Mark Sullivan, "The Flat Tax," *Challenge*, May–June 1996.

13. Robert Eisner, "A Progressive Flat Tax," in Jeffrey Faux, and Todd Schafer, eds., *Reclaiming Prosperity*, Armonk, N.Y.: M. E. Sharpe, p. 83.

14. Dick Armey, *The Flat Tax*, New York: Ballantine Books, 1996, p. 64.

15. Ibid.

5

PUNISHING
THE POOR

A society which reverences the attainment of riches as the supreme felicity will naturally be disposed to regard the poor as damned in the next world, if only to justify making their life a hell in this.

—R. D. TAWNEY, British historian

In the mid-1960s President Johnson and a Democratic Congress declared a "War on Poverty." On one front, this war was waged successfully: because programs such as Social Security, Medicare, and Medicaid were steadily implemented over three decades, the elderly were in relatively good shape in the mid-1990s.

The percentage of people over sixty-five who were poor, which was 24.6 percent in 1970, had declined to 10.5 percent in 1995. Other Americans were also aided in the early years of the "War on Poverty," but after the 1970s they suffered continuous setbacks. In 1996, when President Clinton and the Republicans succeeded in "ending welfare as we know it," millions of Americans lost the meager benefits that had helped stave off hunger and want. Clinton did not acknowledge that the situation of the poorest Americans was significantly worse in 1995, the year before "welfare reform," than it had been fifteen to twenty-five years earlier. This was particularly true for children.

When he was first elected in 1992, Clinton's stated intention was to get welfare recipients into decent, regular jobs while providing for job training, medical care, and day care for their children. He realistically predicted that such a program would cost substantial sums of money. It was a completely different story four years later. Since Clinton was eager to take credit for ending welfare before the 1996 election, he instead signed a Republican bill that took punitive measures against the poor and cut $9.2 billion per year in antipoverty funds. Millions of women and children lost their Aid to Families with Dependent Children (AFDC) income supports; millions more among the working poor were hurt by the biggest single cut, a $4 billion reduction in food stamps; thousands of disabled children were denied Social Security benefits and rehabilitation care.

THE WORSENING CONDITION OF AMERICA'S CHILDREN		
Percentage of Children in Poverty	1970—15%	1995—23%
Percentage of Homeless Who Were Children	1985—27%	1995—39%[1]

Today poor people are being demonized. They have been portrayed as an enemy within, one that is dragging down the whole country. Rush Limbaugh, who set the mean-spirited tone of the first half of the 1990s, complained that "the poor in this country are the biggest piglets at the mother pig and her nipples. . . . They're the ones who get all the benefits in this country." Conservative representatives in the U.S. Congress likened the poor to "alligators" and "wolves" who would devour the rest of society.

Nothing could be further from the truth, but these notions served to assure the self-satisfied rich that their amazing gains in income were nothing compared with the windfall being reaped by the so-called welfare queens. Long before Clinton and Gingrich agreed to mount an attack on welfare,

the War on Poverty had been transformed into a "War Against the Poor."[2] The success of that war is evidenced by their reduced shares of the nation's personal income.

FALLING INCOMES FOR POOR AND NEARLY POOR HOUSEHOLDS[3]			
	1979	1994	% DECLINE
The Poorest 20% of the Population	$10,088*	$8,875	− 12%
The Next 20%	$24,527	$22,151	− 9.8%

*Average household income adjusted for inflation

Abandoning the Poor

The abandonment of the poor began in the early 1980s, when the Reagan administration decided it could no longer afford to promote the general welfare of low-income Americans. Funding for all kinds of social programs began to disappear. Since these spending cuts occurred at the same time as a severe recession, the official percentage of people living in poverty jumped dramatically, from 11.1 percent in 1978 to 15.2 percent in 1983. The rise in poverty was made particularly harsh by drastic cuts in federal expenditures for housing; the subsidy programs of the Department of Housing and Urban Development decreased from $32 billion in 1978 to $10 billion in 1988. Mass homelessness, a phenomenon unknown in modern industrial societies except in times of war or depression, became a common reality in the United States.

The problems of housing were only exacerbated in the 1990s. By 1996, the shortfall in low-income rental units had increased to five million. In New York City alone the number of apartments available to low-income renters fell from 1,170,000 to 691,000 between 1984 and 1996. Meanwhile, the percentage of income that the poorest one fifth of New York's population—well over a million people—spent on rent and utilities jumped from 60 percent to 79 percent. By 1996 Housing and Urban Development (HUD) offices in New York had a list of 336,000 families who were waiting for housing assistance and a six-year backlog of people who had yet to be interviewed. To avoid homelessness, hundreds of thousands of families crowded together; often two or three families were forced to share one apartment. The HUD programs which had financed the construction of millions of units of new housing in the 1970s had been abandoned completely. Congress did not allocate any money for construction of new low-income housing in 1996. Even though there were 15 million families who qualified for federal housing assistance, only 4.5 million actually received help.[4]

NO PLACE TO LIVE		
	NUMBER OF LOW-INCOME FAMILIES	NUMBER OF LOW-INCOME RENTAL UNITS AVAILABLE
1970	7.3 million	9.7 million
1985	11.6 million	7.9 million

The war against the poor was carried on at all levels. State governments were encouraged to follow the example of the federal government, either because they agreed ideologically that the poor should be punished or because their treasuries were depleted of money by the federal cutoffs of funds. Thus state welfare benefits to poor families, AFDC, fell to ridiculous and cruel levels:

THE STEEP DECLINE IN MAXIMUM MONTHLY AFDC*	
1973	1993
$676	$373

*Average of the fifty states adjusted for inflation

These increasingly inadequate levels of support occurred at a time when the percentage of children living in poverty became scandalously high, and far out of line with levels in other advanced industrialized countries:

THE PERCENTAGE OF CHILDREN LIVING IN POVERTY FROM THE LATE 1980S TO THE EARLY 1990S[5]	
United States	21.5%
Great Britain	9.9%
Germany	6.8%
France	6.5%
Belgium	3.8%
Sweden	2.7%

Edward Ziegler, the director of the Bush Center in Child Development and Social Policy at Yale University, offered a grim assessment of the situation: "Children are in the absolute worst status they have been in during my thirty years of monitoring child and family life in this country."

Disparaging the Poor

Rather than come to terms with the difficult problem of supporting children and helping their parents find decent employment opportunities, various political forces found it much easier to attack the moral integrity of the poor. Ronald Reagan had epitomized this trend in his campaign for President in 1980, when he entertained his white, suburban audiences with tales of rip-offs by the poor: "The Chicago Welfare Queen has eighty names, thirty addresses, twelve Social Security cards, and is collecting veterans' benefits on four nonexistent husbands. . . . Her tax-free income is over $150,000." When reporters actually tracked down the real source of the story, they found a woman who had used two addresses to collect twenty-three checks worth $8,000.[6]

Newt Gingrich, the Speaker of the House, used the same kind of misleading exaggeration in 1995 when he lobbied for reductions in SSI, the supplemental security income that helps both disabled adults and handicapped children. He told the U.S. Chamber of Commerce that poor people were coaching their kids in how to fake disabilities and beating them up if they did not succeed. "We are literally having children suffering child abuse so they can get a check for their parents," said Gingrich.[7]

In 1995 there were right-wing think tanks which bolstered Gingrich's rhetoric with grossly distorted data. The Cato Institute, for instance, claimed that average welfare families were earning more than the "working poor" and that they typically received a benefits package equal to $17,500 per year in income. In some places the typical welfare recipients were said to collect as much as $25,000 a year; in Hawaii, they supposedly earned $36,000. The governors of New York and California cited the Cato Institute data when they justified cutting their state welfare budgets. But the figures were too good to be true. The Center on Budget and Policy Priorities analyzed the data in detail and demonstrated that the average welfare family received less than $9,000 per year in benefits, well below the official poverty line.[8]

With their misrepresentation of the numbers, the conservative politicians were suggesting that the nonworking poor were the enemies of the upright, "deserving" poor, those pure of heart who would not ask for help while they labored for miserable wages. The real issue was completely obscured. The distinction between welfare recipients, the working poor, and the nearly poor is a blurred one at best. People in all three categories often live in the same neighborhoods, move in and out of temporary or dead-end jobs with no benefits, and often help each other with child care and emergency shelter. Regardless of what we call them, the poor are much more numerous than the official government poverty levels suggest.

Defining the Poor

Officially, according to the guidelines used by our government, 13.8 percent of the population in the United States, or about 36 million people, lived below the poverty line in 1995. One thing to keep in mind when discussing the number of poor people is that the official poverty levels are exceedingly low. A family of four was considered poor if it earned less than $15,150 in 1995. But, in most parts of the United States, such a family could have earned quite a bit more than $15,150 and still been living in real poverty.

The official poverty-level income did not keep pace with the incomes of other Americans in the previous three decades. In 1960 the original poverty guidelines had set the poverty level for a family of four at $3,022, about 54 percent of median family income, an amount that exceeded the amount of income the American economy produced per capita. Today the poverty line is set at just 37 percent of the median income.

SHIFTING POVERTY LINE			
	MEDIAN INCOME	PER CAPITA SHARE OF GDP	OFFICIAL POVERTY LINE INCOME FOR A FAMILY OF FOUR
1960	$5,596	$2,877	$3,022
1995	$40,611	$27,803	$15,150

If the income at the poverty line were linked to the productive powers of the

American economy (the amount of gross domestic product per capita) in the same proportion as it was in 1960, it would be an astounding $29,315 in 1995, almost twice the level pegged by the government. This figure seems ridiculously high because it comes close to the median income of all American families (remember: the median income has been falling because wages are falling, even though total national income keeps rising). If the poverty line still remained at 54 percent of the median income, it would have reached $21,930 in 1995.

By keeping the income level for measuring poverty at an unrealistically low rate, the federal government has kept the official percentage of poor people between 12 percent and 15 percent of the population. One analysis establishing a realistic poverty measurement for the 1990s was offered by Patricia Ruggles of the Urban Institute. Her figures were tied to food consumption, as were the original poverty guidelines of 1960. Ruggles concluded that 26 percent of Americans were poor.[9]

In their 1992 book, *The Forgotten Americans*, John E. Schwarz and Thomas J. Volgy pointed out that 30 million working Americans who supposedly lived above the poverty line ought to be ranked among the poor. With a wealth of information about the actual expenses involved in getting to work, supporting children, finding housing, and putting food on the table (based on the Department of Labor's estimate of a stringent "low-economy budget"), the two researchers demonstrated that the bare-bones level for staying out of poverty should be set at least 55 percent higher. They showed that if the original concepts for measuring poverty had been maintained, 62.8 million people, 25.6 percent of all Americans, would have been poor in 1989, as opposed to the

official count of 31.5 million, or 12.8 percent.[10] In 1995 about 25 percent of the population, or 66 million people, were poor according to Schwarz's and Volgy's guidelines (a family of four earning $23,483).

The Central Issue: Low Wages

The most immediate cause of poverty is not lack of work per se, nor the insufficiency of welfare benefits, nor the reluctance of people to work, nor the female-headed family, all of which have been offered as explanations. It is, quite simply, the insufficiency of wages. In 1995, about 30 percent of all workers in the United States earned a wage less than the $7.28 per hour which was needed for a full-time, year-round worker to earn the inadequate but official poverty-level income for a family of four. And more than 40 percent of American workers made less than the wage necessary—$9.10 an hour for full-time work—to reach 125 percent of the poverty level for a family of four.

Low wages may be the primary cause of poverty, but they are certainly not the only one. For many Americans, the difficulty is in finding the work in the first place. Sociologist William Julius Wilson, who helped popularize the term "underclass," took pains in his 1996 book, *When Work Disappears: The World of the New Urban Poor*,[11] to point out that the major problem of people trapped in America's inner-city, "underclass" neighborhoods is not the "welfare mentality" or "culture of poverty" attributed to them by upper-middle-class whites, but the simple lack of employment of any kind.

Other researchers have shown that poor people actively seek work when it's available. Surveys by two University of Chicago sociologists, Marta Tienda and Haya Stier, have determined that most inner-city adults in the 1990s were working, and that of the remainder only a few were trying to avoid work. They classified 5 to 6 percent of the inner-city adults they studied as "shiftless" (thus actually giving definition to the derogatory term), but found that the vast majority of the unemployed were merely "jobless." Tienda and Stier also found that among those who would seek work, "black men appeared most willing and white men least willing to accept low-paying jobs." The lowest wage rate that was acceptable to those looking for a job was $5.50 among African-Americans, $6.20 for Mexicans and Puerto Ricans, and $10.20 for whites.[12]

How to Deal with the Poor?

A great many Americans, both liberal and conservative, are under the impression that social spending is breaking the budgets of local, state, and federal governments and that most of this money is being spent on the poor. Nothing could be further from the truth. Richard Sutch, professor of history and economics at the University of California, studied all the funding that is transferred to the public from the government, including such things as Social Security and welfare, and concluded that the amount has actually declined in recent years: social spending consumed 15.7 percent of the gross domestic product in 1976 and 15.4 percent in 1992.[13] And, when he looked at the portion of social spending which actually benefits the poor—rather than middle-income groups—he found that it was getting smaller. Over the last twenty years these public expenditures on the poor declined as a percentage of gross domestic product, from slightly over 2 percent in the 1970s to under 2 percent in the 1990s.[14]

During the Great Depression of the 1930s the United States devoted almost 5 percent of its economy to helping the poor. We are vastly richer now, yet politicians from both political parties in the 1990s insist that we must be stricter with the poor. The day after the Welfare Reform Act of 1996 was passed, Speaker of the House Newt Gingrich claimed that the punitive measures slashing assistance to poor children would be good for them: "I believe this bill will dramatically help young Americans to have a chance to rise and to do better."

At about the same time, Paul Krugman, an economist at MIT, wrote: "In the United States, the crucial thing to remember is just how poor the poor are and how rich the country is. If the United States were willing to devote, say, two percent [of its gross national product] to income supplements for the working poor, the effect would be dramatic."[15] That amount, $150 billion in 1996, would have raised the wages of 30 million people by $5,000 per year, the equivalent of adding $2.50 per hour to their pay.

Such positive approaches to poverty were unthinkable among the political and business classes during the 1980s and the 1990s, because the prevailing conservative viewpoint denied the true extent of poverty and simultaneously inflicted new degrees of social suffering. This malign neglect forced millions of people into the ranks of the poor and the near-poor. It combined with a far more powerful force—the reorganization of work by corporate America—in a process of grinding down American workers and lowering their expectations and self-esteem. When President Clinton and a host of governors pushed former welfare recipients out into the marketplace to compete for lousy jobs with the working poor, a stark new world of work awaited them.

1. Nancy Folbre, *The New Field Guide to the U.S. Economy*, New York: New Press, 1995.

2. The title of an informative book by sociologist Herbert J. Gans on the changing politics of dealing with poverty in the United States: *The War Against the Poor*, New York: Basic Books, 1995. A very good and accessible reference on the state of poor people in the early 1990s has a similar title: *The War on the Poor: A Defense Manual* (by Randy Albelda, Nancy Folbre, and the Center for Popular Economics at the University of Massachusetts, New York: The New Press, 1996).

3. Mishel, Bernstein, and Schmitt, *The State of Working America 1997*, Table 1.6, p. 53.

4. Jason DeParle, "Slamming the Door," *New York Times Magazine*, October 20, 1996, p. 52. For the statistics cited in the chart that follows see Philip Mattera, *Prosperity Lost*, Reading, MA: Addison-Wesley, 1990, pp. 128–29.

5. Lee Rainwater and Timothy M. Smeeding, "Doing Poorly: the Real Income of American Children in a Comparative Perspective," Working Paper No. 127. Syracuse, NY: The Maxwell School, Syracuse University, 1995.

6. Lou Cannon, *Ronald Reagan: Role of a Lifetime*, New York: Simon & Schuster, 1991, p. 518.

7. Molly Ivins, "Mean-spiritedness," Harrisburg, PA: *Patriot News*, April 11, 1995, p. A7.

8. Bob Herbert, "Poison Numbers," *New York Times*, April 22, 1996, p. A13.

9. Patricia Ruggles, "Measuring Poverty," *Focus*, Vol. 14, no. 1, 1992. Her figure falls about midway between the percentage of the poor as determined by historical relation to median income and its relation to per capita income. If the figure of $29,315—which is linked to the productive capacity of the economy—were used, then at least 30 percent of American families would be living in poverty. If we counted those at 54 percent of the median income, as in 1960, we would have approximately the same percentage of the poor, 22–23 percent, as we did then. The reader is cautioned that the definition of poverty changes over time in relation to how the average citizen lives. Economist John Kenneth Galbraith explained thirty years ago why we need to adjust our ideas of poverty to the changing standards of the majority and to the productive capacity of the economy: "People are poverty-stricken when their income, even if adequate for survival, falls markedly behind that of the community ... They are degraded for, in the literal sense, they live outside the grades or categories which the community regards as acceptable." The shame of our time is that a great many Americans, including our political leaders, are quite comfortable with the fact that more and more full-time workers are laboring at poverty-level incomes.

10. Schwarz and Volgy, *The Forgotten Americans*, New York: W. W. Norton, 1992, p. 62.

11. William Julius Wilson, *When Work Disappears: The World of the New Urban Poor*, New York: Alfred A. Knopf, 1996.

12. Marta Tienda and Haya Stier, sociologists at the University of Chicago, cited by David M. Gordon, "Values that Work," *The Nation*, June 17, 1996, p. 22. In New York City, Katherine Newman of Columbia University did extensive research among the working poor of central Harlem and confirmed some of the findings from Chicago. In the "underclass" neighborhood she studied, where 40 percent of the population was living below the poverty line, 67 percent of the households had at least one full-time worker.

13. Richard Sutch, "Has Social Spending Grown Out of Control?" *Challenge*, May–June 1996, p. 12. Medical costs are excluded from this number. See Chapter 18 for more discussion. Health spending, especially Medicare, which serves all older Americans and not just the poor ones, did go up sharply in the public sector, from 2.4 percent in 1968 to 6 percent in 1992; private health spending went up in a similar fashion.

14. Ibid.

15. Letter to *Foreign Affairs*, July–August 1996.

PART

II

6

DOMINATION

BY THE

CORPORATION

The masters of the government of the United States are the combined capitalists and manufacturers of the United States.

—WOODROW WILSON

At the beginning of the twentieth century the public was well aware of where power resided—in the corporate boardrooms—and often protested about the antidemocratic tendencies of big business. The major presidential figures of the era, Woodrow Wilson and Theodore Roosevelt, felt obliged to acknowledge the negative influence of "the monopolies," "the trusts," and people who owned them, "the Robber Barons." Now we find ourselves at the end of the same century and economic power is even more concentrated, but seldom questioned. Common people are not likely to think they have any control over the distribution of wealth in society, and the president of the United States is not prepared to criticize the giant manufacturing, financial, sales, and service corporations for taking control of our destiny. Such an admission would cost him his job.

Big business dominates American society far more than the government could ever hope to. Its positive achievements include raising productivity to the highest rate in the world (that is to say, the average worker produces more value, as measured by the quantity and quality of goods and services, than anywhere else) and created, for the first time anywhere, the possibility of a comfortable, "middle-class" existence for a majority of their working-class employees. In the 1950s and 1960s the five hundred largest corporations (sometimes called the Fortune 500) employed approximately 20 percent of the U.S. workforce. Many of these workers were unionized and could look forward to lifetime employment. They bought their own houses, sent their kids to college, and started building up retirement "nest eggs" in company pension funds.

Over the past two decades the situation has changed dramatically. The biggest corporations still control a huge proportion of the economy, but they offer fewer opportunities—only 10 percent of working Americans now labor for the Fortune 500.[1] Many large corporations—particularly those in the high-paying manufacturing sector—"outsource" their production; that is, more components and services are provided by smaller contracting companies, foreign-based and domestic, which pay much lower wages. Big companies that seek to get rid of unions practice ruthless "downsizing" by cutting their labor forces to the bone. This in turn puts more pressure on the remaining employees to work faster and longer.

A harsh new world of work has emerged: average workers are accustomed to declining wages, while the top managers who instituted the new "lean and mean" production standards expect extraordinary growth in their compensation. *Business Week* reported that the pay of the top executives at Fortune 500 companies averaged $3.75 million per year in 1995, up 30 percent from the previous year and 92 percent higher than in 1990.[2] The profits of Fortune 500 companies had risen 75 percent since 1990, providing stockholders with an unprecedented 14.6 percent return on equity in 1995.

Layoffs of workers by the Fortune 500 were also up sharply, by 39 percent in 1995.[3]

The pay of those workers who remained rose only 2 percent for 1995 and a mere 16 percent from 1989 to 1995. Just to prove this was no fluke, CEOs' total compensation at the Fortune 500 jumped 54 percent in 1996 and profits were up 23.3 percent, surpassing the record of the previous year. Once again millions of employees had nothing to show for their efforts: wages went up 3 percent, lagging just behind inflation.

How Productive Is the Corporate World?

Soaring profit rates and the Wall Street boom have convinced the media that American corporations are doing a terrific job. In some respects this is true. When we look at the biggest companies in historical perspective, they consistently come out as winners. The largest industrial corporations have steadily increased their share of economic activity and the banking corporations have consolidated control even more tightly.

THE ASSETS OF THE 100 LARGEST INDUSTRIAL CORPORATIONS (AS A PERCENTAGE OF THE TOTAL ASSETS OF ALL NONFINANCIAL CORPORATIONS)[4]		
1961	1977	1995
22%	24%	30%

THE ASSETS OF THE 50 LARGEST BANKS (AS A PERCENTAGE OF THE TOTAL ASSETS OF ALL BANKS)	
1980	1995
50%	70%

When the Fortune 500 companies hit the jackpot with record profits in 1995 and 1996, their share of all corporate profits jumped from 43 percent to 48 percent, almost half the profits generated by the hundreds of thousands of U.S. corporations. At the top of the top, business is even more concentrated. Of all the revenue generated by the Fortune 500 in 1996, fully 19 percent was produced by just ten corporations, including General Motors, AT&T, Exxon, Ford, and GE.[5]

Yet, for all this apparent success, it is evident that some things are seriously amiss. CEO pay at the Fortune 500 went up 925 percent from 1980 to 1996, while nonsupervisory workers, who make up four fifths of the American workforce, saw their salaries decline by 13 percent over the same period. CEOs earned 42 times as much as the average factory worker in 1980; they earned 217 times as much in 1996. These changes were accompanied by a strong endorsement of "supply-side economics" within the business and political worlds. Supply-side advocates claimed that the transfer of resources to the rich and powerful was going to unleash a vigorous wave of investment and generate an economic boom. But did reduced taxation on the rich and the corporations enhance the economic performance of the United States in the 1980s and 1990s? The chart below shows that it did not.

The failure of supply-side economics was spectacular. As we have already seen, nothing trickled down to poor and working people. More important, their suffering and sacrifice was all for naught, because the U.S. economy suffered its worst record of sustained growth since the Great Depression.

What happened? The rules of employment and making money have been turned upside down by new forms of corporate dominance. Despite their growing range of economic activity, the corporations are no longer creating and sustaining the kinds of jobs that allow workers and their families to achieve "the American dream." In this section we will review the ways that corporations have expanded their control over American society: the war against workers that parallels the war against the poor; the globalization of production; the corporate pursuit of public monies; and the degradation of business ethics and culture in a "money-takes-all" world.

	THE RANGE OF FEDERAL INCOME TAX ON THE WEALTHIEST AMERICANS	EFFECTIVE TAX RATE ON AMERICAN CORPORATIONS	ANNUAL ECONOMIC GROWTH RATE IN THE UNITED STATES
1950s	84%–92%	26.4%–27.3%	+4.0%
1960s	70%–91%	17.0%–27.3%	+4.4%
1970s	70%	12.5%–17.0%	+3.2%
1980s	28%–50%	9.1%–12.5%	+2.8%
1990–1995	31%–39.6%	9.1%–11.6%	+1.8%

1. "How High Can CEO Pay Go?," *Business Week*, April 22, 1996, p. 101.
2. Ibid.
3. Ibid.

4. Nancy Folbre, *The New Field Guide to the U.S. Economy*, p. 110.
5. *Fortune*, April 28, 1997, and *Economic Indicators*, June 1997.

7

MERGE, CHURN, MONEY TO BURN

If American corporations and wealthy investors did not invest their bonanza of riches in developing the productive capacity of American industry, where has their money gone over the past two decades? Much of it has been used up in a flurry of "financialization" and speculative activity that produced trades and acquisitions, "paper profits," and the redistribution of assets.

In the mid-1980s, large funds of capital were amassed and used to finance mergers among the giant companies. In 1985, just eight corporate mergers (and there were many more) used up an amount of capital equal to one third of the money that was invested in the productive capacity of the entire American economy. Among these deals were: the GE takeover of RCA; the General Motors purchase of Hughes Aircraft; the R. J. Reynolds acquisition of Nabisco;

and the U.S. Steel abandonment of the steel business in favor of Texas Oil and Gas.

Tax breaks for corporations, like tax incentives for individuals, were supposed to encourage investment in new production, but instead they helped to increase the rate of takeovers. By using various kinds of accounting methods to manipulate the losses of acquired companies and the expenses involved in the acquisitions, many large corporations avoided paying taxes.

This kind of spending continued through 1988, the year that a record $353 billion was spent on corporate mergers. At the same time a similar kind of speculation, also fed by the large pool of lightly taxed financial resources, was rampant in the savings and loan and commercial banking industries. Vast overinvestment in real estate, both commercial and residential, was caused by falling capital gains taxes and highly accelerated depreciation (itself the result of new laws that allowed investors to write off the value of their income property twice as fast as before). All of the speculative excesses—whether in corporations, banks, or real estate—helped deplete the economic resources that were necessary to counteract the cyclical downturn, or recession, that was overdue by the end of the 1980s. Thus the next six years, 1989 through 1995, were a period of very slow economic growth.

By 1995 and 1996, with the economy starting to recover, the merger fever picked up again (this time without the competition from real estate). Companies went on another record-setting spree of consolidation, investing $518 billion on mergers and acquisitions in 1995 and over $600 billion in 1996; mergers were especially brisk in telecommunications and media stocks, as well as in health care, aerospace and defense, insurance, and banking. Monopolization of business was seldom opposed by the antitrust division of the Justice Department; for instance, after some initial questioning, it approved the $23 billion merger of Bell Atlantic and NYNEX in 1997, even though the new company was sure to dominate the market for telephone service in the Northeastern United States. Others saw concentrated ownership as economic efficiency at work. Peter Solomon, a New York banker, voiced the typically enthusiastic reaction of the investment community: "All this is leading to massive consolidation, making American business as strong as ever, and leading to lower prices for consumers."[1]

This round of oligopoly affected almost every economic sector, including the aerospace/defense industry, where huge companies had long predominated. The top ten corporations had folded into just three megagiants by 1997: Boeing, Lockheed, and Raytheon. The same thing was happening in areas where large-scale corporate control had previously seemed unlikely. In the staid, solemn, otherworldly realm of funeral homes, one company, Service Corporation International, became so big that it offered $3.1 billion in 1996 to buy out its chief funeral chain rival. The idea was to create a new company with globalizing pretensions; it would own a combined 3,750 funeral homes and 600 cemeteries (British and Canadian operations included) and perform one of every seven funerals in the United States. Would this deal bring efficiency and lower prices to consumers? The previous record of the Service Corporation said otherwise; almost everywhere it had gone into business, it ended up dominating the market and pushing up the price of funerals by 20 percent.

Investors Seize the Day

Defenders of capitalism often claim that the market economy is "democratic" because ownership is open to everyone. Many American families do participate in stock ownership; a Federal Reserve report in 1995 showed that 15 percent of households owned shares directly (down slightly from 17 percent in 1992) and that an increasing number, 41 percent, participated in the stock market indirectly, through investment in mutual funds, pensions, and retirement accounts. Those who praise "stockholder democracy" claim that bold interventions by leading investors, be they very rich individuals or the managers of well-endowed pension funds, have forced corporations to be more accountable for their actions.

The implication is: 1 person, 1 share, 1 vote. Which sounds democratic until one hears the other side of the equation: 1 person, 5 million shares, 5 million votes. Of all the shares of stock held directly, through individual ownership, the wealthiest 1 percent of Americans control 71 percent.[2]

The millionaire and billionaire investors who own the big stakes in American business were once characterized, during the prosperous years of the 1950s and 1960s, as idle sorts who sat back clipping their coupons and passively watching their wealth grow. Nowadays some big stockholders are aggressively involved in active investing, challenging the top corporate managers over the direction of various companies. Often they push for short-term gains in place of long-term strategies of sustained production and technological development.

The 1980s, with their excessive emphasis on quickly realized capital gains, spawned new breeds of capitalists such as "corporate raiders" and specialists in "leveraged buyouts." Big-time players such as T. Boone Pickens and the firm of Kohlberg, Kravis, Roberts, & Co. (KKR) would identify an undervalued stock and capture a controlling interest in the company. Then they would instruct management to sell off valuable chunks of the company or otherwise remix the corporate structure in a process known as "churning." Certain big corporations contracted in size as they were forced to spin off high-performance divisions in ways that would profit stockholders immediately in the form of higher dividends, stock splits, or direct cash sales.

In the late 1980s and early 1990s, the pressures from potential raiders forced many companies into financial strategies for increasing short-term profits and pushing up the value of their stocks to avoid being bought out. Kirk Kerkorian, who amassed an unusually large percentage of Chrysler Corporation stock (13.75 percent), did not succeed in getting the company to disperse its long-term savings to shareholders, but he did manage to push the value of his stock upward by $2.9 billion by threatening to buy out the whole company. KKR was still busy buying and selling in the 1990s, too. Taking advantage of a trend toward concentration in the insurance industry, they invested $300 million in a leveraged buyout of American Reinsurance in 1992, only to earn $2 billion by selling it to a giant German multinational in 1996. A month after that deal, KKR was cashing in on another nicely engineered acquisition, this time in brand-name commodities; the firm took home $2.4 billion when Gillette paid $7 billion for the Duracell Corporation.[3]

The overemphasis on quick earnings and lifting the value of their shares on the stock market often encouraged managers to engage in massive layoffs in all sectors of their corporations. The banking sector was no exception to this trend. When Chase Manhattan and Chemical Bank were consolidated into the nation's largest financial institution in 1995, the new company immediately laid off 3,600 employees, thus producing an exceptionally good profit rate of 18.7 percent in its first three months.

Who Will Tell the Story?

Americans interested in stories that document the concentration of wealth and power within the corporate structure will seldom find them in the mainstream media. This is because the information industries, which prefer to report breathlessly about the exciting world of business, have been monopolized at a remarkable pace in the past two decades and are now immensely profitable corporations themselves.

In 1981, forty-six media companies controlled most of the book, magazine, newspaper, movie, and television industries. By 1986, this number had shrunk to twenty-nine and by 1989 to twenty-five. Then, in the 1990s, the process of conglomeration in the media was so rapid that one could scarcely follow the players. Disney bought ABC, Westinghouse bought CBS, and General Electric took over NBC. A new network, Fox, was able to supply some competition, but only because it was part of a huge global newspaper, book, and TV empire belonging to Rupert Murdoch. Time/Warner not only controlled magazines, movies, and books, but had also taken over Turner Broadcasting, CNN, and a wide swath of the cable TV distribution network.

By 1997, just seven giant companies had nearly cornered the vast multimedia markets of the United States: Rupert Murdoch's News Corporation, Viacom, Time/Warner, Newhouse, General Electric, Westinghouse, and Disney. Newspaper monopolies such as Gannett and Knight-Ridder keep enlarging their chains at the expense of the last independent city papers. Some foreign behemoths such as the German Bertelsmann corporation, the world's second-largest media company, moved swiftly into the American book and recording markets; other giants from abroad—such as the Dutch companies Elsevier and Wolters Kluwer and the French Hachette Filipacchi corporation—are worldwide leaders in periodicals and now publish a great many American magazines and academic journals.

The concentration of economic resources in a few individual and corporate hands is thus matched by a similar domination of information and ideas. The larger business community wants regular access to media sources in order to broadcast favorable information—that is, advertising—within an engaging and inoffensive format. Advertising

revenues, because they pay for all of commercial TV and radio and most of newspaper production, make the media shy of attacking other big business interests.

While they are unlikely to be critical of the products or employment policies of their advertisers, the media behemoths are by no means sitting on their hands. Often—as in the case of ABC, which is owned by Disney—the news apparatus is a small department of one division, the television network, that fits within a much larger entertainment corporation. So when the company wants to celebrate its biggest assets, it devotes TV news time and other programming to the event. This "synergy" allowed ABC's *Good Morning America* to devote an entire two-hour show to Mickey Mouse in Orlando on the twenty-fifth anniversary of Disney World.

For those who never trusted the quality of information transmitted by television in the first place, there is even more disturbing news from the world of books. In the 1980s and 1990s, most large and midsize independent publishers were bought up by multimedia conglomerates which saw the prospect of big profits where they had never existed before. André Schiffrin, a longtime managing director of Pantheon Books (before it was swallowed up by Random House), explained that the average profit margins for the publishing industry had been about 4 percent from the 1920s into the 1980s. When the independent publishers were bought up by the multimedia corporations, the new owners expected "the high returns they demand from other subsidiaries like newspapers, cable television, and film. New profit targets have therefore been established in the range of 12 to 15 percent."[4]

The new giants of publishing concentrated their energy on "blockbusters"—popular romance and suspense novels by big-name authors or memoirs by movie stars and public figures—that could be marketed by their other media outlets. Appearances on Oprah, or Leno and Letterman, were considered a necessity for giving name recognition to authors, and publishing budgets were directed toward million-dollar book advances for the "stars" of the writing world. When HarperCollins (part of Murdoch's News Corporation) paid English novelist Jeffrey Archer a £32 million advance (about $50 million), it was a warning sign that the book industry had been transformed into something akin to the other entertainment media. Layoffs of editorial staff at the London offices of HarperCollins were attributed to the inordinate size of Archer's advance; this was followed by massive downsizing of the publishing lists at HarperCollins in New York. The company simply canceled the contracts for hundreds of books in 1997 (a tactic that was legal, but almost unheard of previously). This was a signal to other big publishing outfits that they ought to trim their mid-list books—the name for offerings by noncelebrity authors in serious fiction, history, criticism, and other genres that used to be published regularly in modest printings that brought in modest profits.

In a very short period U.S. publishing had become dominated by a small group of conglomerates which then proceeded to narrow the product line and restrict the employment opportunities of the primary producers (the writers and editors). But did they know what they were doing, even in a pure business sense? In 1997 the publishing industry was faltering: the book retailers (now dominated by corporate chains of superbookstores) were returning unsold books in record numbers and the overall sales of hardcover books were down by 8 percent.

1. Charles V. Bagli, "MCI Deal Would Speed Pace of Current Mergers," *New York Times*, November 2, 1996, p. 37.

2. Poterba and Samnick, "Stock Ownership Patterns," *Brooking Papers on Economic Activity*, vol. 2, 1995, p. 326. Figures date from 1992, so may have dipped slightly due to the mutual fund craze.

3. "Some Accused of Insider Trading in Duracell," *New York Times*, September 17, 1996, p. D6.

4. André Schiffrin, "The Corporatization of Publishing," *The Nation*, June 3, 1996, p. 30.

8

THE WAR AGAINST WORKERS

Labor is prior to, and independent of, capital. Capital is only the fruit of labor, and could never have existed if labor had not first existed. Labor is the superior of capital, and deserves much the higher consideration.

—ABRAHAM LINCOLN, in his first
annual message to Congress, 1861

Today the abstract value of capital—personified in the form of capitalists and executives who think of themselves as "stars"—comes first. Capital has very little consideration for labor or the people who supply it. The corporate executives who dominated the mid-1990s put up some impressive numbers and were duly rewarded. One of the big numbers was layoffs:

• Frank A. Shrontz, CEO of Boeing, laid off 25,000 workers and was paid $5.9 million, up 73 percent.

• Robert F. Daniell, chairman of United Technologies, earned $11.2 million after overseeing the dismissal of 30,000 employees in the previous five years.

• "Chainsaw" Al Dunlap fired 11,200 workers while at Scott Paper Co., merged the firm with Kimberly Clark, and moved its headquarters from Philadelphia to Boca Raton, Florida. For eighteen months' work he was paid $100 million. "Did I earn it?" wrote Dunlap in his book, *Mean Business*. "Damn right I did. I'm a superstar in my field, much like Michael Jordan in basketball and Bruce Springsteen in rock 'n roll."[1]

The top managers who specialized in lay-offs felt that their stellar gamesmanship was bringing in billions of dollars in revenue for shareholders, so they were not embarrassed that these riches were gained at other people's expense. On the contrary, said Professor Peter D. Cappelli of the Wharton School of Business, "Today a CEO would be embarrassed to admit he sacrificed profits to protect employees or a community."[2]

A corporate compensation consultant confided to the *Wall Street Journal*, "Most CEOs won't cut their pay merely because it's 200 times higher than the guy at the bottom. The people who own the stock don't care about the gap."[3] That is, if profits are soaring, shareholders could care less about workers.

The big news in 1995 and 1996 was that corporate America had made a comeback. The rates of profit had never been higher, productivity was up, and, according to many media reports, prosperity for ordinary Americans could not be far behind. If good jobs were hard to find, the upbeat appraisal went, then people would have to try harder to educate themselves for employment opportunities, because the new, "streamlined" corporate world was too fast and nimble to wait for malingers; working people, whether white or blue collar, had better be fast and nimble themselves.

In the 1980s the giant companies spent so much on merger madness that they neglected to attend to their real duty: rebuilding American industry. But, at the same time, American wages were falling low enough in comparison with those of other advanced industrialized countries that by the 1990s, manufacturing was looking much more profitable in the United States. Manufacturing wages were 20 percent higher in Japan and 60 percent higher in Germany. Foreign companies noticed the growing wage differential. Japanese auto producers such as Toyota, Mitsubishi, and Nissan established shiny new production facilities in the United States in the 1980s, and by 1994 were producing more cars within the U.S. than they shipped in from Japan. Some of these automobiles were exported to Europe, a few back to Japan itself. In the 1990s BMW and Mercedes-Benz decided to build their expensive sedans in South Carolina and Alabama because they could pay much lower hourly wages than those demanded by the metalworkers' union in Germany.

But what about American-owned industry? In the 1990s U.S companies had realized they could do what foreign industrialists were doing in the United States: by taking advantage of lower wages, they could keep prices down, thereby increasing profits and making their products more competitive on the world market. Industrial production began to rebound and the business press was ecstatic: "America Ascendent: U.S. Companies' New Competitiveness" read a headline in the *Wall Street Journal*.[4] According to *Business Week*, the U.S. economy was "riding high," productivity was "soaring," and corporations were not downsizing, they were "right-sizing."[5]

This celebration of U.S. corporations by the media was pure hyperbole. According to Robert H. Hayes, professor of business administration at Harvard University, the media were engaging in "feel-good journalism."[6] The nation's productivity (the amount of goods and services actually produced per hour of work) had grown at the anemic annual rate of 1.3 percent between 1990 and 1995,[7] only marginally better than the 1 percent rate of the late 1970s through the 1980s, and nothing compared with annual rates of 3 percent and more achieved from 1948 to 1973. The reason, explained

Hayes, was that investment in plant and equipment had been low. When he compared the investments of the 1990s, which were 2 percent of corporate revenues, with those made before 1980, he found that companies were reinvesting at only one third the rate of the earlier decades.[8] Corporations, intent on increasing profits by paying labor less, were not developing the technology and workplace innovations that can simultaneously raise wages and productivity.

Benjamin Harrison, one of America's most careful observers of industrial organization, described the prevailing business attitude: the corporate world was not merely aspiring to be fit and agile, it was getting "lean and mean."[9] Harrison supplied answers to the troubling conundrum posed in the last chapter: how is it that the largest five hundred corporations are increasing their share of economic activity when they are now employing fewer people than ever?

The answer is that these companies are changing the nature of work in America. In many instances, they avoid hiring permanent workers, preferring instead to rely on "contingent" workers, including temporary employees, who are hired for much lower pay and benefits than long-term workers. Furthermore, large corporations choose to "outsource" much of their production to a network of subcontractors, whose wages and benefits are grossly inferior. The industrial giants have placed themselves at the center of global networks that depend on production from a variety of suppliers with lower profit margins. A dual economy, within the United States and across the world, calls for two kinds of labor: higher wages at the center of the network—for management, marketing, research and development, and a few highly skilled production tasks—and lower wages everywhere else.

In the automobile industry, Ford and Chrysler have been particularly effective at cutting jobs in their own facilities while buying more and more supplies from nonunion, low-wage producers within the United States and Mexico. In 1996, the *Wall Street Journal* reported that General Motors, which was not as profitable as its major rivals despite having laid off 99,400 workers from 1992 to 1996, was looking for ways to vastly increase its outsourcing of parts and components.[10] Within the United States, GM could not resist the idea of undercutting the base wage of unionized autoworkers, $20.69 per hour, by contracting with suppliers who paid $11 per hour or less. At the time, GM was spending 45 percent of its North American manufacturing dollars in its own plants, versus 38 percent for Ford and a mere 34 percent for Chrysler.[11] According to an auto industry consulting firm, this meant production savings to Ford of $440 per vehicle, and to Chrysler of $600, over GM's costs.[12]

Increasingly, the auto giants are cultivating networks of highly competitive, small, independent parts manufacturers. These companies, domestic and foreign, have virtually eliminated unions in their ranks over the span of twenty years. In the 1970s, two thirds of auto parts suppliers' employees were union members; by 1996 eight out of ten were nonunion.[13]

Just as significant a development are the strategies which large corporations pursued within their own factories. At the beginning of the 1980s, they took advantage of a severe recession and an increasingly antiunion political environment to attack blue-collar workers directly. Management cut wages, imposed repeated layoffs, and reduced company contributions toward health insurance coverage and pension plans. Although some companies which were struggling to survive may have done this out of desperation, most simply recognized the opportunity to lower the labor component of their manufacturing costs. The Diebold Corporation, the largest producer of automatic teller machines, is a case in point. Even though the company had been able to increase its dividends to share-holders for forty-three consecutive years, it started putting pressure on its Canton, Ohio, workers in 1984, a time when jobs were dis-appearing all over the Midwestern "Rust Belt." Diebold demanded and received long-term wage concessions from eight hundred unionized workers in return for keeping pro-duction in Ohio; as a result the hourly pay for an assembler fell (in constant dollars) from $11.83 in 1983 to $9.93 in 1996.

The company reneged on its part of the bargain, however, by building new produc-tion plants in Virginia and South Carolina and employing nonunion labor there. By 1996 the average pay in Canton, where wages had been cut, was still 51 percent higher than in the South, but only fifty-eight union workers remained. The CEO of Diebold, Robert Mahoney, was handsomely rewarded for his efforts: his pay went up almost 500 percent, to $2.37 million per year, from 1990 to 1995. And his example did not go unnoticed by other manufacturing companies in the same Ohio county. In June of 1996 the Hoover Company, the highly profitable vacuum cleaner division of May-tag, gave its unionized workers a choice: allow newly hired workers to receive only $7.50 an hour in a plant which had been paying an average of $14.50, or the plant would go to Texas. The workers refused; the company moved.[14]

As mentioned, Japanese and German com-panies took advantage of the antilabor envi-ronment and built plants for Honda, Toyota, Nissan, and BMW cars in southern Ohio, Tennessee, and South Carolina. (Mercedes-Benz and Volvo also moved into the market for big trucks.) Like American companies, they usually chose to locate their factories in the Sun Belt states, far from the established and unionized centers of auto production. They were not unlike our own corporations in another way: managers were accountable to investors who lived very far away. It hardly mattered whether they resided in New York, London, Frankfurt, or Tokyo.

During the 1980s and 1990s, a startling shift occurred that altered the manufactur-ing balance between the states. Many of the southern states, which feature low wages and "right-to-work" laws discouraging unionization, are now in the top ranks of manufacturing. That is, they have a higher percentage of employed people who work in manufacturing than other states, including the old labor bastions of the North, such as Michigan and Pennsylvania. North Carolina lists 26.6 percent of its workers in manufac-turing, Mississippi 26.1 percent, and South Carolina 24.2 percent. Only Indiana has a higher rate, at 27.2 percent, and that rank is sustained, in part, by the fact that it alone among northern states has right-to-work laws. The poorest, seemingly least developed states, Mississippi and Arkansas, which rank forty-ninth and fiftieth in almost every eco-nomic category, are contenders for highest percentage of manufacturing workers (26.1 percent and 21.2 percent), challenging the old industrial stalwarts, Michigan (23 per-cent) and Pennsylvania (23.3 percent).

In the past, low wages and suppression of unions were sufficient to attract certain low-tech industries to the South, in particular textile manufacturers, which long ago moved their operations out of New England and the mid-Atlantic states. Now, in order to lure more production their way, state and local governments practice "corporate welfare" on a scale rivaling the most obeisant of third world countries. They promise to provide free job-training services and a wide variety of generous tax breaks in an effort to persuade companies to set up shop within their borders. The most spectacular giveaways were promised to foreign automakers. Alabama beat out North and South Carolina for a new Mercedes-Benz plant by putting together a $300 million package of subsidies, which included $5 million annually for employee training. This did not include the extras that were thrown in later: calling out National Guard troops to clear the construction site for free and agreeing to buy $75 million worth of new four-wheel-drive Mercedes vehicles as official cars for state employees.

Corporations of all kinds, not just those in manufacturing, have become highly successful in their efforts to intimidate local governments. In 1995 New York City offered tax deals worth $30 million each to the financial firms Morgan Stanley and Kidder, Peabody, and Company so they would not leave Manhattan. Anaheim and the state of California promised $800 million worth of civic improvements on behalf of the Disney Corporation when it threatened to move Disneyland to a more friendly location. Raytheon, the biggest employer in Massachusetts, bargained for an annual tax break of $20 million per year from the state in return for not moving jobs to Tennessee and Arizona. Once it had the agreement in hand, it proceeded with downsizing its Massachusetts operation and cut forty-five hundred jobs.[15]

Downsizing, Top to Bottom

Downsizing remained popular with investors through the mid-1990s, because it indicated the company was putting their interests before those of workers. A company needed only to announce sizable layoffs and its stock prices jumped on Wall Street. When Sears said it was trimming fifty thousand jobs in 1995, its shares rose 4 percent the same day; when Xerox cut ten thousand workers, its stock was instantly worth 7 percent more.[16] The week that Chase Manhattan and Chemical announced their merger and the layoff of thirty-six hundred employees in 1995, the stock of both banks went up 11 percent.[17]

David Shulman, a chief equity analyst at the Salomon Brothers investment house, noted, "There is competition for capital between the real economy and the financial economy." A business columnist for the *New York Times* followed up with this explanation: "The real economy includes everything from new machinery and new manufacturing plants to new homes, but it does not include the financial markets. So when the real economy slows down—when people aren't shelling out money to buy things—the money thus freed up can slosh over into the financial economy, driving up prices for stocks and bonds. . . . So for now, at least, there is no quicker way to get your stock price up than to announce plans to fire a lot of workers."[18]

Unlike the labor squeezes of the 1980s, which mostly affected unionized blue-collar workers with high school educations, the downsizing of the 1990s targeted managerial, service, and sales workers. These people were unlikely to belong to unions and many were likely to be college-educated, middle-aged, and, in some cases, high earners. The *New York Times*, *Time*, and *Newsweek* ran articles sympathetic to the plight of the more privileged, salary-earning workers (who probably come closer to the demographics of their readership). Many of these people, who thought they were entering their prime earning years, were faced with the prospect of downward mobility for the first time in their lives.

Fifty-year-old ex-managers, who would learn that most companies thought they were no longer employable, were not the only ones to feel the pinch. Younger middle managers who remained on duty lived in constant fear of dismissal. When United Technologies rewarded Robert F. Daniell with $11.2 million in compensation for laying off thirty thousand employees, the average area manager with twenty years of experience was expected to make the hard choices and implement both blue- and white-collar layoffs, then produce more with a leaner workforce. These managers were not rewarded with a share of the rising company earnings (up 28 percent in 1995); their salaries stayed in the comfortable, but not extravagant, range of $64,000 a year. They were just happy to be the ones left with jobs.[19]

The employment landscape in the mid-1990s was an eerie one. General Motors was still in second place among the nation's largest employers, with 705,000 workers. But it had been surpassed by an unlikely candidate, the temporary employment firm Manpower, which was sending 767,000 people out to work every day so that other corporations would be spared the cost of filling permanent positions. The next two largest employers behind General Motors epitomized the low-wage, nonunion service economy that has come to dominate the country: Wal-Mart discount stores employed 675,000 workers and PepsiCo, with its fast-food chains, had 480,000 employees.

Wal-Mart typifies the dilemma of a society propelled by consumerism and courted by corporate retailers. Most of us shop at Wal-Mart or at other similar chains such as Kmart because we can get bargains on many basic things that we need. On the other hand, when Wal-Mart moves into a community, the downtown shops and small businesses close up and the retail profits, which once went to store owners and remained in town, are now shipped to corporate headquarters in Arkansas. The company pays poverty-level wages of between $5 and $7 to local citizens, many of whom are desperate for any full-time employment that supplies health insurance, as Wal-Mart does. In 1994, for instance, Wal-Mart moved into Greenport, N.Y. (less than one hundred miles up the Hudson from New York City). At the time, the country was supposedly in the middle of an economic recovery, and only 5 percent of the people in the area were listed as unemployed. Nevertheless, over 1,600 people rushed out to apply for the 172 full-time and 73 part-time positions.[20] In such places, the government often provides indirect subsidies to Wal-Mart and the other low-cost retailers, because their employees receive such low pay that they are eligible for public assistance in the form of food stamps and housing allowances.

Furthermore, Wal-Mart serves as a major purveyor of low-wage products from abroad, especially the flood of shoes, clothes, and toys produced in China. In certain cases Wal-Mart, along with other major retailers, has earned notoriety for marketing clothes produced under sweatshop conditions in the United States and abroad. Government inspections of labor sites in the United States have become so infrequent that thousands of illegal manufacturing operations paying far less than the minimum wage have been able to spring up in California and New York. In New York City, according to the General Accounting Office, only fourteen labor inspectors were assigned to track down and monitor forty-five hundred sweatshops employing more than fifty thousand people. Public indifference to low wages and the problems of low-wage labor was finally shaken by publicity campaigns mounted by American unions. Workers testifying about inhuman working conditions in Honduras and New York were able to embarrass celebrities, such as TV talk host Kathie Lee Gifford and supermodel Kathy Ireland, who were paid to have their names marketed on Wal-Mart clothing. The company, like many other retailers, sought refuge from bad publicity by claiming it had no way of knowing which companies were making its clothes. Low-wage labor and oppressive working conditions are on the increase inside and outside the United States, but no one wants to admit responsibility for them.

1. Albert J. Dunlap, *Mean Business: How I Save Bad Companies and Make Good Companies Great*, New York: Times Books, 1996, p. 21.

2. "How High Can CEO Pay Go?," *Business Week*, April 22, 1996, p. 103.

3. Ibid.

4. The *Wall Street Journal*, August 9, 1994.

5. *Business Week*, October 9, 1995.

6. Robert H. Hayes, "U.S. Competitiveness: 'Resurgence' vs. Reality." *Challenge*, April/May 1996, p. 37.

7. According to two Federal Reserve economists, Stephen D. Oliner and William B. Wascher: "Is a Productivity Revolution Under Way in the United States?" *Challenge*, November–December 1995.

8. Hayes, p. 37.

9. Benjamin Harrison, *Lean and Mean: The Changing Landscape of Corporate Power in the Age of Flexibility*, New York: Basic Books, 1994, p. 299.

10. *Wall Street Journal*, April 26, 1996.

11. John Lippert, "Suppliers and Demands," *In These Times*, July 8, 1996, p. 26.

12. Keith Bradsher, "What's New at G.M.?," *New York Times*, September 8, 1996, Section 3, p. 10.

13. John Lippert, p. 26.

14. Michael Winerip, "Canton's Economic Seesaw: Managers' Fortunes Rise as Workers Get Bumpy Ride," *New York Times*, July 7, 1996, p. 10.

15. Allen R. Myerson, "O Governor, Won't You Buy Me a Mercedes Plant?," *New York Times*, September 1, 1996, Money & Business pp. 1 and 10.

16. "The Lost Job and the American Dream in Reverse," *New York Times*, March 3, 1996, p. 28.

17. Floyd Norris, "You're Fired! (But Your Stock Is Way Up)," *New York Times*, September 3, 1995, p. E3.

18. Ibid.

19. "How High Can CEO Pay Go?," p. 101. The point about the area managers conforms with income data in Chapter Two: although they were paid a decent middle-class income of $64,000 per year in 1995, having had 4 percent raises from 1993 through 1995, they were in no way partaking of any of the financial gains that the company earned through downsizing.

20. Jacques Steinberg, "Retail Giant Becomes a Job-Seeker's Oasis," *New York Times*, January 19, 1994, p. B1.

9

LABOR DISCIPLINE: TAKING IT OUT OF THEIR HIDES

Speeding them up and grinding them to pieces, and sending for new ones
—Upton Sinclair, *The Jungle*, 1906

A frightening transformation has taken place over the past three decades. Overall economic productivity increased, so that by 1994 the income per capita in the United States was 53 percent higher than it had been in 1967. Yet the real hourly take-home pay of a worker who earned the median income actually declined by 4 cents.[1] Most American workers have been unable to enjoy the fruits of their labor. And the organizations which represented labor, and once had battled on behalf of workers, are rapidly disappearing.

Once, at the midpoint of the twentieth century, organized labor had stood tall in

PERCENTAGE OF THE AMERICAN WORKFORCE REPRESENTED BY UNIONS	
1953	1996
36%	14.5%

America and was generally accepted as a legitimate partner—albeit a junior partner—of business and government in determining national goals and social priorities. Labor's status had been recently won, the result of years of hard-fought struggles that culminated in the National Labor Relations Act of 1935, which gave workers the legal right to bargain collectively and go on strike. In the late 1930s massive and militant sit-down strikes in the rubber and auto industries launched a wave of unionization that swept through American industry.

Workers succeeded in winning dignity and a fair share of the economic pie after six decades of being on the losing end of industrialization and economic modernization in the United States. From the end of the Civil War through the 1920s, a host of unions and pro-labor movements—including groups such as the Knights of Labor, the American Railway Union, and the Industrial Workers of the World—were repeatedly crushed by a coalition of businessmen and government officials. For instance, when workers went on strike at Andrew Carnegie's colossal steel plant in Pittsburgh in 1892, the state militia of Pennsylvania, armed with machine guns, was called in to subdue the strikers. The steelworkers' union did not reappear for decades. Much later, even after the National Labor Relations Act was passed, remaining outposts of the antilabor coalition could still muster brutal means of intimidation. In the Hilo Massacre of 1938 in Hawaii, police shot down fifty supporters of a multiracial union which was organizing sugar and pineapple workers.

When labor ascended to a position of respectability and power, roughly from 1945 to 1975, there was an era of unusual harmony between unions and corporations. Companies expected to earn a regular profit and most working people took home paychecks that rose each year at the rate that the economy expanded. There were still disagreements and strikes, but they were generally settled under the supervision of the National Labor Relations Board, a federal, nonpartisan body appointed by the President and charged with guaranteeing fair bargaining by both labor and business.

This all began to change in the late 1970s, when business decided to mount a relentless drive to diminish the power of organized labor. The defining moment signaling that government would take the side of business came in 1981, immediately after Ronald Reagan took office as President. He fired all the federal air traffic controllers, whose union, PATCO, was staging a nationwide strike to protest that working conditions were too stressful, and thus too dangerous for the traveling public. PATCO was completely destroyed by the President's actions and thousands of new controllers were hired at vastly reduced wages.

U.S. corporations took their cue from the President and began an assault on working Americans. They started campaigns to decertify existing unions and to prevent the certification of new unions. They engaged in countless unfair actions against existing unions with the assurance that the National Labor Relations Board, which had been packed with antiunion members by President Reagan, would not rule against them.

In the early 1980s unionized workers faced a multitude of increasing pressures. The effects of a long economic recession were exacerbated when Reagan imposed severe cuts in federal spending on social programs in 1981 and 1982; then industrial corporations, especially in the northern states, began to lay off huge numbers of workers. Workers were forced into "givebacks"—meaning they gave up gains in pay, benefits, and working conditions that had been won in previous years—by corporations that threatened to close down or move factories to different states or other parts of the world. In 1982 union members had to accept wage cuts or freezes in 44 percent of the contracts negotiated (meaning their wages could not keep up with inflation). This was in stark contrast to the previous two decades, when organized labor had almost never given such concessions.

When the economy turned upward in 1984, the political climate was distinctly probusiness, and unions were not in a position to fight back. Corporations had invested heavily in an array of antilabor "consultants." By the 1990s, two thirds of all American companies facing unionization had hired antiunion consulting firms; they spent $2 billion per year employing seven thousand lawyers and other advisers to help disorganize their workers. In one out of four U.S. companies, employees were fired for engaging in pro-union activities.[2]

The resubjugation of labor involved establishing a programmatic reversal of the gains made by workers in the mid-twentieth century. Corporations sought to:

• reduce hourly wages

• reduce benefits, such as health insurance coverage, and eliminate cost-of-living adjustments

• reduce or eliminate health and safety regulations in the workplace

• induce older, better-paid workers to accept a two-tiered wage plan, whereby new and younger workers have to accept much lower starting salaries

• institute grueling speedups and overtime schedules

• create more nonunion workplaces, since unions are consistently shown to produce higher wages and better benefits for their members

The Cost to Workers = The Profit to Owners

American corporations did not wage this battle for nothing. Owners of capital realized that they could increase their return, not by investing in higher productivity, but by decreasing the union "premium" on wages. In-depth studies have demonstrated that unionized blue-collar workers enjoy wages 50 percent higher than those of nonunion workers; their total compensation, because they bargain vigorously for health insurance and other benefits, is 68 percent higher. Some observers have argued that this advantage merely reflects the historical gains made by workers in a minority of privileged industries, but this is largely untrue. Even when union workers are compared with others of comparable experience—by region, education, type of industry, occupation, years of employment, marital status, etc.—the union premium is still high, providing 20 percent more compensation than nonunion work. This figure holds true, with only minor variations, for men and women of all races.[3]

Obviously, corporate management can easily calculate the pay and benefit advantages in a particular industry and then determine how to profit by doing away with organized labor. By extracting concessions from blue-collar workers in the early 1980s, corporations restored profitability to more than 7 percent between 1984 and 1986. (It had fallen from 10 percent in 1965 to 6 percent in 1977.) Then, with the implementation of downsizing measures against all employees, that profit rate was pushed up throughout the 1990s; by 1995–96 it was well over 10 percent, matching the all-time highs of the mid-1960s.

Clearly, labor's defeats made things more difficult for the surviving unions, whether they were negotiating contracts for existing members or reaching out to the unorganized. Furthermore, nonunion workers lost a hidden advantage when unions were stamped out. In the past, in areas with substantial union activity, the managers of nonunion firms would frequently offer raises and improved working conditions in order to prevent organization within their plants and offices. Now, as the fortunes of union workers declined, so did the opportunities of the unorganized.

Back to the Jungle

In 1906, Upton Sinclair wrote *The Jungle* in order to describe the cruel realities of American industrialization, in particular in the meatpacking industry, which treated people as if they were animal carcasses, "speeding them up and grinding them to pieces, and sending for new ones." Ninety years later the United States, after seemingly eliminating that kind of exploitation, had come full circle.

Once again meatpacking companies instituted some of the worst wage cuts and working conditions of any industries. A few giant firms—IBP, Cargill, and Con-Agra—controlled 80 percent of all beef production and a large share of the pork market. In 1983 Con-Agra bought thirteen plants from Armour, one of the old meatpacking giants, and lowered the pay of three thousand workers from $10.69 to about $6 per hour. Average pay in another factory in Iowa in 1981, just before IBP took over, was $30,000 per year. The company cut wages for new workers to $6 per hour in 1982; in 1996 that wage had risen only barely, to $7 per hour, or about $14,500 per year. Throughout the industry, hourly pay fell by 31.4 percent over fifteen years when adjusted for inflation. Meatpacking workers, who used to earn more than the average manufacturing worker, now earn almost $3 an hour less than the average manufacturing employee—

whose wage has itself declined significantly over the same time period.

Compounding this bad situation, there were drastic and dangerous speedups on the assembly line. By 1985 one representative factory was running its "beef chain" 84 percent faster than in 1979; consequently there was a parallel 76 percent increase in injuries to workers. Data from another plant show this practice continued into the 1990s. "Chain" speed increased 125 percent from 1969 to 1994, to a pace so grueling that it resulted in a turnover rate in employees of 83 percent per year. Meatpacking had become the most dangerous industry in the United States; in 1996, according to *U.S. News & World Report*, 36 percent of all employees were injured. In order to keep up a steady stream of replacement workers, companies in Iowa and Nebraska recruited illegal workers in Mexican villages and brought them north. In 1996 Nebraska state officials estimated that illegal migrant workers represented 25 percent of the meatpacking workforce.[4]

The ability of companies to bring in low-wage labor enhanced their power to exploit the workforce in general. Upton Sinclair described the same phenomenon at the beginning of the century—"the people had come up in hordes," he wrote—when millions of impoverished Americans streamed into the cities from rural areas and southern states. At the end of this century, some Americans feel threatened by immigration from places even farther to the south, but the more potent and real danger to the livelihood of workers in the United States originates elsewhere.

As we have seen, U.S. corporations have responded to workers' most effective form of protest, the strike, by moving to non-union locations within our own country. Today companies use the additional threat of moving outside the United States and utilizing a web of international production that depends upon even more egregious exploitation of wage earners, often under the supervision of repressive foreign governments.

1. David M. Gordon, *Fat and Mean*, New York: The Free Press, 1996, p. 20.

2. M.E. Sharpe, "Labor's Future," *Challenge*, March/April 1996, p. 66.

3. Mishel, Bernstein, and Schmitt, *The State of Working America*, pp. 119–20.

4. "The New Jungle," *U.S. News & World Report*, September 23, 1996.

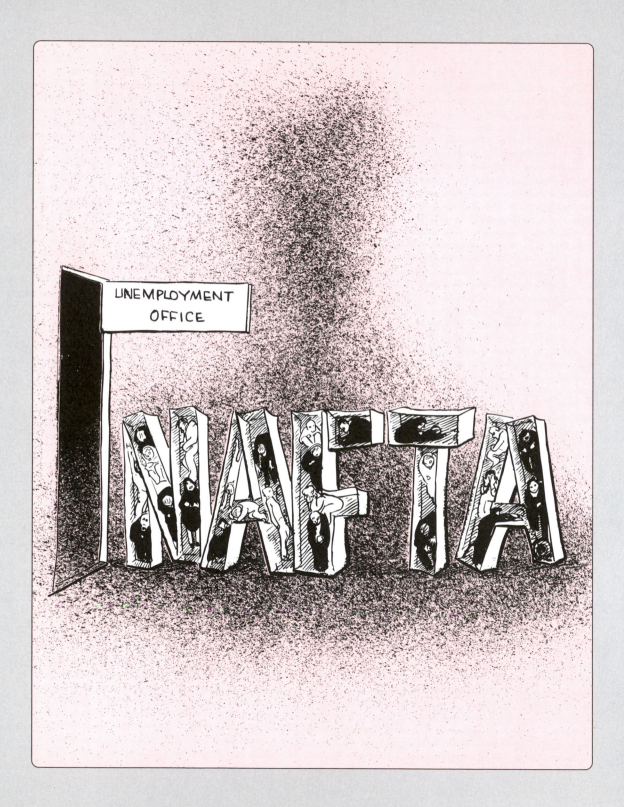

WHERE HAVE ALL THE GOOD JOBS GONE?

American companies have either shifted output to low-wage countries or come to buy parts and assembled products from countries like Japan. The U.S. is abandoning its status as an industrial power.

—AKIO MORITA, cofounder and chairman of
Sony Corporation, quoted in *Business Week*, 1986

At the end of the 1980s the last television factory operated by an American company in the United States was sold to the Korean corporation Samsung. After two years, it shut down the factory, one of the few places in Camden, New Jersey, that could offer its workers even the modest wage of $9 per hour. Samsung had invested $212 million in a spanking-new, high-tech facility in the Mexican border town of Tijuana, where it paid its workers slightly over $1 per hour, or $50 for a forty-five-hour week. By 1996 the TV factories in Tijuana alone were employing as many people as all the television factories left in the entire United States (which were all foreign-owned).

When Akio Morita criticized the behavior of the biggest American corporations, he was only half right. As we have seen in previous chapters, the corporations not only shifted output to foreign lands, but also happily relocated their industries to cheap-labor areas at home. Today, Morita would have to admit that Japan and other nations have also been drawn into the process of globalization. Japanese corporations have been seeking cheaper production sites all over Asia, and on other continents as well. The Sony corporation itself set up shop in Nuevo Laredo, a city of maquiladoras (factories for assembly and export into the United States) near Texas. In 1994 the company fired eighteen workers who were trying to organize a union, then called in Mexican riot police, who beat the remaining workers and forced them to return to their jobs. The United States government could have used the labor provisions of the newly enacted NAFTA (the North American Free Trade Agreement) to take action against Sony.[1] It did not.

Moving Next Door

Even as U.S. corporations and banks were spending vast sums of money monopolizing economic life within the United States, they were also managing to pour billions into industrial plants in foreign countries where laborers toil for extremely low wages. In doing so they contributed to a foreign trade situation that turned disastrous for the U.S. in the 1980s. Exports from the U.S. declined by 2 percent between 1980 and 1986, while imports into our country increased by 51 percent. Many of the imports were produced by foreign companies, but a great quantity, amounting to 40 percent of all imported merchandise, was manufactured by the foreign subsidiaries of American transnational corporations. This kind of activity explained a sudden change in the auto trade between the U.S. and Latin America:[2]

AUTO TRADE IN REVERSE		
	1981	1986
U.S. Auto Exports to Latin America	$3.6 billion	$2.7 billion
U.S. Auto Imports from Latin America	$0.8 billion	$4.2 billion
Auto Trade Balance	+$2.8 billion	−$1.5 billion

The arrangement was neatly described by the American director of a new high-tech auto facility in Mexico: his engines, he bragged, were the product of "U.S. managers, European technology, Japanese manufacturing systems, and Mexican workers."[3] In this equation, which produced profits for U.S. capital, U.S. workers were left out.

U.S. operations in Mexico were disadvantageous for Mexican workers, too. When General Motors built a new production plant in Ramos Arizpe near the U.S. border, the most important geographical consideration was setting up shop far from Mexico City, where a strong labor union exerted its influence. Consequently GM was able to pay its Mexican workers just 50 to 60 percent of the prevailing wage in Mexico City, while making them work seven or eight hours longer each week.[4] General Motors was slipping into second place in employment in the United States (behind the temp employer Manpower) but it had become the largest private employer in Mexico.

High-paying U.S. jobs were lost in this process; furthermore, the profits which U.S. multinational companies earned from their foreign ventures did not necessarily return to the United States. In the early 1990s, when General Motors was losing part of its share of the American market, it was getting its biggest earnings from its European operation, which produced the increasingly popular Opel models. Business logic would tell us that some of the profits from European production were probably reinvested in Mexico, not in the United States. Or that GM would introduce the same strategies it had put to such good use in Mexico in its European operations. Which is exactly what it did. General Motors decided to locate its newest German factory in the former East Germany because it could pay wages and benefits amounting to 40 percent or less than those paid in the western part of the country.[5]

Many big investments by the American auto industry in Mexico came before the North American Free Trade Agreement was ratified. Although NAFTA would make it even easier for U.S. companies to take advantage of cheap Mexican labor, the pressure of wage differentials was already intense in 1991. Labor economist Harley Shaiken reported that Ford paid its skilled laborers in its Hermosillo factory $2 per hour in wages and benefits, as opposed to the prevailing rate of $30 per hour in Detroit.[6] When NAFTA was passed in 1993 with the concurrence of both Republicans and Democrats, it merely gave a well-established corporate process the seal of approval from the United States government. Prior to NAFTA ratification, the value of the Mexican peso had been jacked up by the Mexican government with the approval of Mexican businessmen and U.S. investment bankers, who were eager to maximize the profits on cross-border takeovers and mergers. When the peso threatened to collapse entirely in 1994, the U.S. bailed out the banks and the Mexican government to the tune of $50 billion. The peso was devalued and the Mexican worker's already miserable wages were effectively cut in half.[7]

By 1996 the Clinton administration had to admit, contrary to its claims that NAFTA would create more U.S. jobs, that seventy-five thousand U.S. workers had lost employment as factories moved to Mexico. Labor groups thought the figure was far higher, but more important than the dispute over just how many jobs shifted was the clear evidence that there was a huge change in the balance of trade. In 1992 the United States had enjoyed a trade surplus of $5.4 billion with Mexico; by 1995 the flood of Mexican imports had produced a $15.4 billion trade deficit for the United States.[8] This did cause a boom in jobs along the U.S.–Mexican border, where the maquiladoras were employing an additional five to six hundred thousand more Mexicans and paying lower wages than ever. But the increased employment in one part of Mexico was more than offset by other NAFTA effects: the falling peso and the disintegration of the nationally owned sectors of the Mexican economy caused a loss of 1.4 to 2 million jobs throughout the rest of the country.[9]

Finding Cheap Brainpower

The transfer of business by transnational companies involves much more than moving technology to low-wage areas that can provide high-intensity labor. Today corporations will transplant almost any kind of production, including their highest technology, highest-skill jobs, to Mexico and other developing countries. The Cummins Engine Company, which operates over fifty factories worldwide, rated its plant in San Luis Potosí as the most successful at adopting new production techniques. High-end production jobs are often followed by high-end conceptual work in engineering and design. Hewlett-Packard chose the Mexican city of Guadalajara as the site of its new, world-class product design center in the Western Hemisphere. Its design center on the eastern side of the globe opened in Singapore.[10]

In the high-tech realm, American companies are heading out of the United States in order to maintain their market edge. Cypress Semiconductor, the world's largest producer of computer semiconductors, has downsized its Silicon Valley factories in favor of opening new facilities in Bangalore, India, and in tax-free zones near Manila. In 1996 Cypress was guaranteed that there would be no taxes and no labor unions for the first eight years of operation in the Philippines. Plenty of low-wage labor for its assembly lines was available, at about $5 per day, but the more interesting employment opportunities concerned the engineers who would run the factories—in the Philippines, an English-speaking engineer with five years' experience can be hired for $8,000 per year. The situation is the same in India, which graduates a hundred thousand engineers from its universities each year. The cost of employing one of them is one sixth or one seventh that of hiring a similarly qualified engineer in the United States.[11]

T. J. Rodgers is the corporate "star" at the helm of Cypress, a man relentlessly pushing the bottom line on behalf of his stockholders. He is amply rewarded with multi-million-dollar contracts and bonuses, and he is also uncommonly honest. When pressed to offer a rationale for drastic downsizing in one of the U.S.'s most successful high-tech businesses, he said: "The world is free-market capitalist." And when asked why an American worker was better off because of these global changes, Rodgers replied: "He's not. You can't save a job that doesn't have an economic right to exist."[12]

In the early 1990s, there was a lot of noise from economists, including then–Secretary of Labor Robert Reich, to the effect that undereducated American workers were losing out to their better-educated brethren, the so-called symbolic analysts who had the skills to compete in the twenty-first century. A quick look around Bangalore reveals the shallowness of such an argument. Not only have IBM, Hewlett-Packard, and Texas Instruments taken up residence and hired local technical talent, but one Indian entre-preneur set up a company called Infosys Technologies Limited, a state-of-the-art office complex staffed by 1,150 engineers. The engineers plug into fifteen hundred computer workstations that allow them to provide individualized reports by satellite to various companies in the United States and Europe. Since the clock in India runs about half a day ahead of North America's, these engineers can have their reports downloaded into the offices of clients in the United States before the workday has even begun there.[13]

Infosys and companies like it may or may not succeed in displacing Americans from their "symbolic analyst" jobs, but their existence foreshadows the coming wave from the East: India is said to have one hundred thousand software engineers, and China at least three hundred thousand.[14] Soon most mathematicians and a majority of scientists in a number of fields will be Indian or Chinese; many of them are already rising to prominence in American and European universities. In cultural terms this should be a positive development, deflating the haughty pretensions of "Western culture." But in economic terms, as the situation is exploited by transnational investors, it could speed up the demise of good jobs in the U.S., as well as America's status as the leader in high-tech research.

The CEO of General Electric, Jack Walsh, went to India in 1989 to set the stage for outsourcing much of his company's software and technical work. The findings from his trip were summed up in a corporate memo: "The cost of living in India, about one-sixth that of the United States, provides capability for extremely cost-effective solutions." The other half of the solution, massive layoffs at GE in America, followed soon thereafter.[15]

Leanness and Meanness, International Style

We live in an era when free trade is trumpeted as the defining virtue of Americanism. American capital is free to travel to any part of the world in search of maximum profit, and foreign capital is encouraged to do likewise in the United States. In the process, American citizens encounter and purchase a never-ending flurry of products—Japanese cars, Chinese clothing, Mexican cars and clothing—which are driving our merchandise trade deficit higher than ever, to nearly $200 billion in 1996.

Among the products Americans purchase in great quantity from factories operated abroad are athletic shoes, first and foremost those with the Nike label. The Nike company is American-owned, mostly by its founder, Phil Knight, who is said to be worth more than $5 billion. Nike combines low-wage and low-tech production with the most sophisticated high-tech marketing and distribution of goods. It produces sneakers at a cost of about $5.60, materials and labor combined, then sells them for $73 to $135 per pair all over the world. Nike, based in Oregon, has no U.S. production facilities and depends entirely on fast, high-dexterity, low-pay labor abroad. The company scours the world to find subcontractors who pay the lowest possible wages. Until the early 1990s, most Nikes were assembled by subcontractors in South Korea and Taiwan. When wages rose too much there, twenty factories were closed. Thirty-five new ones were opened, often under Korean and Taiwanese ownership, in Indonesia, Thailand, China, and Bangladesh. In 1991 an experienced female worker in Indonesia earned 82 cents per day; others made much less.[16] Indonesian workers who sewed Nikes told

a reporter from the *Far Eastern Economic Review* that they were "terrified" of their South Korean managers, who often threatened them.[17] Others told the *New York Times* that Korean supervisors "liked to hit people, slap people. There were some who would kick the Muslim workers when they were praying during their lunch break."[18]

Because of international pressure, Nike fired the subcontractor who operated that particular Indonesian factory; by 1996 Nike was managing to pay the legal minimum wage, which had risen to a little over $2 per day. Journalist Bob Herbert asked Knight why he didn't pay higher wages to the workers in Indonesia. Herbert reported the interesting answer: "He said it would wreck the country's economy if wages were allowed to get too high."

In the meantime Nike began slowing down its Indonesian expansion because it was pursuing cheaper options with its subcontractors in China, which now produces almost one half of all the world's shoes. One gigantic new Chinese factory complex in YuYuan employs forty thousand workers, 70 percent of them women. Each immense building at the site is emblazoned with a major brand name—Nike, Reebok, Adidas, L. A. Gear—and inside production is carried out to the exact specifications of that particular Western company. Outside the plants, it is possible to witness one of the strange paradoxes of multinational production: foreign managers, brought in from Taiwan (where many were once officers in the Taiwanese army), scream out orders and march new recruits around in military formation. Workers live in newly constructed barracks—ten to a room is considered relatively low-density housing—and perform twelve-hour shifts. The workplaces resemble prisons. At another South China plant, this one owned by Taiwanese investors, one hundred guards are employed to make sure that no one escapes the premises.[19]

In the North China city of Tianjin, the Korean-run factories are even more harsh. According to sociologist Anita Chan, managers resort to "beatings, military control, and public humiliation" to keep their workers in line. Of the ten labor strikes that occurred in Tianjin in 1993, nine were against Korean operations. The Chinese authorities who respond to labor unrest and complaints are not necessarily sympathetic to their own citizens. In addition, many officials in the trade unions are retired officers from the Red Army, and their highly regimented training makes them poor arbitrators of workers' complaints. "The common underlying belief," writes Anita Chan, "that they and the Taiwanese and Korean managers share is not in Confucianism but militarism and authoritarianism."[20]

Taiwan and South Korea are two of the "Asian Tiger" economies that have been the marvel of the industrialized world and the envy of other developing countries. In the 1970s and 1980s, they rose to prominence as Newly Industrialized Countries (NICs) thanks to strictly authoritarian governments that suppressed any sign of labor activity. Their regimes kept wages low and profits very high, in part through their willingness to permit the highest rate of industrial accidents and deaths in the world; at one point in the 1980s it was calculated that 2.26 percent of South Korea's labor force sustained serious injuries or died at work every year. Taiwanese employers vied with the South Koreans for the dubious distinction of requiring the longest workweek in the world.

Working people fought back. In 1988, after a nominally democratic government was installed in South Korea, there was a wave of strikes and fourteen hundred unions were formed. Korean companies retaliated with a vengeance, using well-organized gangs of thugs called Kusidae to terrorize workers and drive out the new unions. One American company, a subsidiary of the Tandy Corporation (the corporation that makes Radio Shack equipment), used these antilabor squadrons to subdue its female workforce. Groups of male Kusidae assisted male managers in the factory in a brutal attack on women union leaders; several women were hung upside down, beaten, and sexually molested; twenty-three others were physically abused in other ways until they signed resignation letters.[21]

Such viciousness was a sign of business "realism"—that is, knowing what to do to boost profits and promote growth in an increasingly competitive world. After four decades of political and labor repression, pressures from the restive working and middle classes eventually pushed both Taiwan and South Korea toward democracy. The new labor unions negotiated successfully for substantial raises that more closely reflected the productivity of the South Korean economy. And, after free elections were held, public anger against two ex-presidents was so great that they were convicted of crimes against the people and thrown into prison.

The traditions of authoritarian repression that once propelled South Korea and Taiwan toward economic success are still alive; they have been eagerly assumed by other regimes in Southeast Asia. Countries such as Thailand, the Philippines, Malaysia, and Indonesia are being pulled into the international web of export manufacturing and are trying to achieve very rapid economic growth under severely antilabor regimes.

These management techniques can be

transplanted to places outside of Asia. In Guatemala five hundred export factories have opened up over the past fifteen years in order to take advantage of the lowest wages in Central America and the disciplinary methods of a repressive government. At these production facilities, half of which are Korean-owned, the most common complaint of workers is that they are yelled at and beaten by their employers. One Guatemalan manager excused the Korean companies' actions by explaining that "the people are accustomed to being treated badly; if you don't treat them badly they don't understand."[22] Wendy Diaz, a fifteen-year-old worker at Global Fashion in Honduras, testified to the U.S. Congress that she had to work seventy-four hours per week for 40 cents an hour. Her South Korean managers, who were accused of hitting and sexually harassing employees, were overseeing the manufacture of clothing for Wal-Mart.

The Boomerang Hits the United States

As tempting as it is to blame our economic problems on rising imports from low-wage nations, we can now find the same sorts of abuses here at home. Some of the worst examples have been found in the sweatshops that employ legal and illegal immigrants and flourish in the New York and Los Angeles metropolitan areas. The most infamous of these was the "slave labor" compound set up in 1988 by Thai and Chinese émigrés in El Monte, California. When labor inspectors finally investigated in 1995 after seven years of operation, they found seventy-two Thai workers in a small compound of houses surrounded by a ten-foot wall topped with barbed wire. The immigrants were required to work seventeen-hour days for as little as

60 cents an hour. The clothing they sewed was routinely sold by wholesalers to premier department stores such as Neiman Marcus, Dayton Hudson, and Hecht's. The company, called D&R Fashions, was able to do business until 1995 because most garment workers in the United States now work in small establishments which are seldom ever seen by U.S. Department of Labor inspectors, who are overworked and understaffed due to government cutbacks.[23]

As scary as the El Monte stories are, the most profound impact of foreign-owned businesses is on high-wage, not low-wage, production. A number of state governments are trying to lure the world's most prestigious manufacturers into the U.S. by offering the same kinds of advantages that developing countries offer. Alabama and South Carolina succeeded in getting Mercedes-Benz and BMW to open their first North American automobile factories by granting them huge tax breaks and providing a cheap and docile labor force that was unavailable in Germany. Alabama gave out $300 million in various incentives, which amounted to a government investment of about $200,000 per job, for a factory that would employ about fifteen hundred people. South Carolina won over BMW with $130 million in tax concessions for a plant that cost between $250 to $300 million to build.[24] Just as important as free cash to the German automakers were the local wages. Starting at around $12 per hour for loudly advertised nonunion labor, wages were less than half of Germany's prevailing rate of $28, and well under the Detroit level of $20 per hour.

In 1993 Alabama business leaders were so proud of the state's achievement that they hoisted a giant Mercedes-Benz ornament over the football stadium before a big game between the University of Alabama and

Tennessee. The gesture symbolized the intense competition among southern states for the dubious honor of having the most antilabor, probusiness policies in the United States. Tennessee is now regarded as the hub of a new, lower-cost auto industry, and South Carolina has established itself as the king of government enticements by successfully luring 185 non-American companies inside its borders.[25]

Clearly the United States has created an unusual kind of "competitive marketplace." It allows European and Japanese companies to compete by paying workers here less than they have to pay at home. Meanwhile the U.S. competes in a different league in the developing world, profiting from systems of authoritarian labor discipline. This kind of double-edged competiveness has exacerbated the woes of American workers and contributed to the mounting U.S. losses in international trade.

For years financiers, industrial managers, and government officials from the United States defended their collaboration with emerging capitalist countries run by authoritarian military regimes, usually on the grounds that successful economic development was more important than short-term problems with the human rights of working people. U.S. trade representatives and bankers scurried around to implement the new wave of industrialization, especially in Asia, and experts from the World Bank and the IMF pronounced the economies of South Korea, Thailand, and Indonesia worthy of emulation throughout the rest of the world. The corrupt military dictatorships that flourished in all three countries allowed for high profits by industry, both domestic and foreign, due to the suppression of unions and democratic opposition; but they also encouraged vast overinvestment in economic schemes cooked up by rich cronies and family members of the military leaders.

Suddenly, at the end of 1997, the stock markets and banking systems of these nations were at the brink of collapse and the monetary systems of Asia and the whole world were severely shaken. The shift in the attitudes of the Western business press was abrupt: the "Asian tigers," which so recently had been praised for producing such high rates of profit, were now castigated for sloppy lending practices and the failure to adopt the public accountability of "democratic" capitalism as practiced in the United States and Europe. The IMF had to arrange gigantic emergency loans to prevent the battered economies from going bankrupt and to reimburse major international banks in the United States for billions of dollars in ill-considered loans. The biggest losers were the poorly paid working people of Asia, who faced massive layoffs as thousands of industries had to close down.

1. David Bacon, "Laboring to Cross the NAFTA Divide," *The Nation*, November 13, 1995, p. 574.

2. "Jobs and Trade," *Economic Notes*, November–December 1987.

3. Philip Mattera, *Prosperity Lost*, Reading, MA: Addison-Wesley, 1990, p. 176.

4. Rhys Jenkins, *Transnational Corporations and the Latin American Auto Industry*, Pittsburgh: University of Pittsburgh Press, 1987, p. 222.

5. Noam Chomsky, "The Masters of Mankind," *The Nation*, 1993.

6. Harley Shaiken, "Transferring High Tech Production to Mexico," *Columbia Journal of World Business*, Summer 1991, p. 130. Shaiken, a University of California professor, has written both scholarly studies and popular articles that

chronicle the move of high-technology industry from the U.S. to Mexico.

7. Brian Burgoon, "The Job-Eating Villain," *Dollars and Sense*, July–August, 1996.

8. Ibid.

9. Sarah Anderson, John Cavanagh, and David Ranney, "NAFTA: Trinational Fiasco," *The Nation*, July 15–22, 1996, p. 27.

10. Robert H. Hayes, "U.S. Competitiveness: 'Resurgence' vs. Reality," *Challenge*, April–May 1996, p. 43, and Richard Barnet and John Cavanagh, *Global Dreams*, pp. 318–20.

11. Harry Smith, "Who's Getting Rich and Why Aren't You?" CBS Special Report, August 8, 1996.

12. Ibid.

13. Ibid.

14. Hayes, p. 44.

15. Barlett and Steele, 1996, p. 99.

16. Barnet and Cavanagh, p. 326.

17. Adam Schwarz, "Running a Business," *Far Eastern Economic Review*, June 20, 1991, p. 16.

18. Bob Herbert, "Trampled Dreams," *New York Times*, 1996, p. A27.

19. Anita Chan, "Boot Camp at the Shoe Factory," *Washington Post*, November 3, 1996, pp. C1 and C4.

20. Ibid.

21. Pharis Harvey, "No Justice for Workers in Korea," *Democratic Left*, September–October 1990.

22. Jane Slaughter, "Inside Guatemala's Maquiladoras," *Labor Notes*, December 1995, p. 8.

23. "Officials Call for Crackdown on Garment Work Conditions," *Washington Post*, September 10, 1995, p. A12.

24. Barlett and Steele, p. 305.

25. Barnet and Cavanagh, p. 321.

THE TRIPLE
DEFICIT SCARE:
REAL OR IMAGINED?

n the 1990s political and social analysts wrote numerous stories about the precarious state of the American economy. Often the villain of the piece, the wolf at the door, was "The Deficit."

The question was: which deficit?

1) Did they mean the Budget Deficit—caused by the profligacy of the federal government—which hit a record $320 billion in 1991?

2) Or were they referring to the Deficit-to-Come, a monstrous shortfall in Social Security funds that would swallow up the whole economy by the year 2047?

3) Or was it the Foreign Trade Deficit that Americans should fear most?

At various points during the past decade, all three deficits have been trotted out as an excuse to attack a host of government programs. When they are real, deficits may indicate something about the weaknesses of our economy. And, even when they are imaginary, the would-be deficits tell us quite a lot about how the interests of private business and the rhetoric of public policy-making converge to set the political agenda.

The Foreign Trade Deficit: Real

Throughout the twentieth century, until 1979, the United States exported more than it imported, thus enjoying a trade surplus; the trend was for both imports and exports to increase each year as international trade became more vigorous. Suddenly, in the 1980s, imports began to exceed exports, and in less than twenty years, a large trade deficit would become a regular occurrence for the United States.

ANNUAL U.S. MANUFACTURING TRADE DEFICITS				
1979	1987	1991	1995	1996
$1 billion	$170.3 billion	$122.7 billion	$173 billion	$200 billion

Foreign imports were not the crux of the problem, for the trade deficit was caused by our inability to export manufactured goods. The value of exports from the U.S. to other countries fell precipitously during the Reagan years, from about 7.8 percent of the gross national product in 1982 to slightly over 5 percent in 1986. Meanwhile imports stayed at about the same percentage of GNP, about 8.5 percent.

In the 1980s U.S. companies trying to compete abroad were hurt by the artificially high value of the dollar compared with other currencies. The dollar rose in value when the Federal Reserve Board decided to help banks and wealthy Americans by keeping interest rates high. The Federal Reserve policies had two negative effects on U.S. exports: the dollar made our goods too expensive for foreigners to purchase; and the high rates of interest in the United States discouraged American companies from making the kinds of long-term investment necessary for maintaining a strong export trade.

When the dollar finally did readjust to lower levels in the late 1980s and early 1990s, falling 40 percent to 60 percent against the stronger mark and the yen,[1] many American manufacturers were able to increase their volume of foreign exports, but the overall situation did not correct itself. American purchases of high-quality goods, especially from Europe, leveled off; but the manufacturing imports from low-wage, industrializing countries began to make up a larger part of our trade deficit. Trade with developing countries accounted for 42.3 per-

cent of all imports into the United States in 1992, up from 27.6 percent twenty years earlier. American companies began to import more and more parts and supplies from low-wage countries and to use them to manufacture goods here in the U.S. Such imports more than doubled in twelve years, from 5.1 percent in 1978 to 10.9 percent in 1990. By the summer of 1996 these trends had allowed China to temporarily displace Japan as the biggest contributor to the U.S. manufacturing trade deficit, at more than $3 billion per month.

As indicated in the previous chapter, many transnational corporations based in the United States continue to invest in high-tech production outside of the country. At the same time, the percentage of the U.S. gross domestic product devoted to private industrial research and development has dropped sharply in the 1990s, falling below 1.5 percent, a much lower amount than expended in other advanced industrial nations.[2] Thus, even as corporations rack up record profits, they shy away from spending on basic scientific research. Japanese companies working in the United States have taken advantage of the situation: six of the ten most frequent filers of patent applications at the U.S. Patent Office in Washington are now Japanese companies. This may help explain why three out of four of our biggest exports to Japan are not manufactured goods, but lumber, unmilled corn, and fish. (To be fair, our largest export to Japan is high-tech: commercial aircraft.)[3]

The trade deficit is problematic for the United States because it suggests that production abroad is an acceptable alternative to creating good jobs at home. In some corporations, more resources are now devoted to marketing budgets than to actual production costs. As goods produced in low-wage developing countries come to represent an ever-larger percentage of all consumer purchases, more American manufacturers consider moving to these countries. When private investment of U.S. companies abroad reached a record $146 billion for the year 1993, the amount equaled two thirds of the net private investment by American companies at home. This not only affects the creation of good jobs, but—as we noted in the previous chapter—puts pressure on the workers who still have jobs in the U.S. to conform to a new international wage scale. For instance, the Xerox Corporation told its workers in Webster, New York, that they had to accept its proposal—50 percent lower wages for newly hired employees—or the company would move its factory to Mexico. The workers complied, because this was no idle threat: Xerox had already closed plants in Illinois and Massachusetts and reopened them south of the border.[4]

The Budget Deficit: Real and Imagined

Throughout the 1980s and the early 1990s, our government focused on ways to enrich the few while burdening taxpayers with trillions of dollars of debt. The total accumulated deficit of the United States from 1789 until 1981, a period of 192 years, was $829 billion. The additional budget deficit accumulated over the following twelve years of the Reagan and Bush administrations was $3.192 trillion.

When the Reagan administration cut taxes on the rich, it also began spending much more money on the military. There were immediate consequences: when defense spending increased by $62 billion between 1981 and 1983, it was accompanied by a budget deficit increase of $59 billion.

The budget deficit grew from 2.7 percent of the gross national product in 1980 to 5.2 percent in 1986 to 6.3 percent in 1991. As the annual deficit kept increasing, hitting a high of $320 billion in 1991, the interest paid on the federal debt became a large burden itself, amounting to about $200 billion per year that had to be paid out of tax receipts. The increases in military spending and the huge interest payments accounted by themselves for all the annual increases in the deficit.

The fact that the federal deficit loomed over our economy for more than ten years was due to political choices, not economic necessity. Not only were conservative forces anxious to decrease the tax burden of the monied classes, but they were also intent on piling the social costs on the backs of the lower classes. "Balance the budget" became a slogan repeated endlessly by both political parties, and it was the primary justification for all kinds of reductions in government services and investments.

In reality, the budget deficit did not prove to be an insurmountable burden. Once defense spending was slowed down and upper-bracket taxes were increased slightly in the first half of the 1990s, the yearly deficit figure was lowered by two thirds in five years, to about $107 billion in 1996. With the stock market boom pushing up tax revenues in 1997, the budget deficit dropped to $40 billion or less. Still, the fear of deficits had been firmly planted in public discourse, so much so that President Clinton gladly joined the Republicans in passing the Balanced Budget Agreement in August of 1997. The provisions of the bill, which granted such favors as capital gains tax breaks and college tuition credits, also required fresh cuts in social spending on top of the massive reduction in assistance to low-income

Americans that had been imposed by the Welfare Reform Act of 1996. The President claimed that the "entitlement savings" stipulated for Medicare would amount to more than $400 billion over a period of five years. The overall aim of the agreement was for the federal government to officially "balance the budget" by the year 2002. At the news conference held the day after the budget bill was signed, Clinton bragged that "we now expect the deficit . . . not only to reach balance by 2002, but to have a surplus in excess of twenty billion dollars."

This bordered on the absurd. The out-of-control deficits of the 1980s had presented a problem, one that had been corrected. But what, exactly, was wrong with a moderate budget deficit? Northwestern University economist Robert Eisner, in his books *The Misunderstood Economy* and *How Real Is the Deficit?*, has tried to get Americans to look at economic processes without getting hysterical.[5] Deficits, he pointed out, are not necessarily disasters. A government deficit may be a problem that is easily remedied, or it may actually show that the country is planning for the future and marshaling its resources by spending on both fixed capital and human capital. That is, like a home owner or a business, the government may be borrowing money now in order to invest in projects that take a long time to pay for. In the end the whole society will own the assets of such projects—be they schools, roads, canals, airports, etc.—and will be richer, not poorer, for having financed such growth. Eisner argues that government, like business, ought to treat such contributions as capital investments, not losses.

Thus, as we look back at the 1980s, one development that was just as alarming as the failure to collect taxes from the rich was that so few public expenditures were directed toward "infrastructure," the basic physical capital of our nation. The roads and bridges, school buildings, mass transit and airports, water and sewer systems, and all the other public property that helps insure economic growth and stability in the future were neglected. Thus federal, state, and local governments were prevented from carrying out one of their most basic functions.

PUBLIC SPENDING ON INFRASTRUCTURE AS A PERCENTAGE OF THE GROSS NATIONAL PRODUCT[6]			
1950s	1960s	1980s	1990s
2.5%	2.3%	0.4%	0.9%

One of the haunting legacies of the "deficit hawks" is the notion that the nation should not borrow money to expand its capabilities, even though the population and economy are growing bigger and the needs of people change. The movement toward the Balanced Budget Amendment was based on a flawed understanding of economic development. The idea that we should reduce the deficit to zero, because otherwise the government will go bankrupt, is ridiculous. The United States government has many trillions of dollars' worth of assets, and the 1997 budget deficit was very low as a percentage of gross domestic product. It stood at just 4/10ths of 1 percent of GDP before the budget agreement was enacted; at the same time, other major industrialized nations in Europe were aiming to reduce their deficits to 3 percent of GDP, a level that is considered financially prudent.

The Social Security Deficit: Imagined

Once the public had been primed to regard any debt as potentially disastrous, it was easy for certain lobbying groups to fan an even more baseless deficit scare. Social Security has been an immensely successful program which has lifted millions of elderly Americans out of poverty. Generally credited with being efficient and responsive to the people it serves, Social Security paid out benefits of $317 billion in 1994 to 43 million people while incurring administrative costs of only 0.8 percent.[7] Because Social Security supplies 55 percent of elderly Americans with over half of their income, it is the primary way in which the United States reduced the poverty rate among people over sixty-five from 35.2 percent in 1959 to 10.5 percent in 1995; the latter figure marks the first time it was ever lower than the rate among working-age Americans.

Social Security taxes are collected from the payroll contributions of all employees and employers. In recent years these contributions have produced a surplus of $50 to $60 billion per year for the federal treasury. As mentioned in Chapter Four, the government has tapped into these excess funds instead of increasing income taxes on the rich. Nevertheless, Social Security is well situated to meet its annual payouts for the next fifteen to twenty years (more than can be said of any other taxation program).[8]

Yet for all the successes of Social Security, it has been attacked vigorously by both conservatives and liberals. According to its detractors, thirty years from now aging baby boomers will be homeless in the streets, thanks to the free-spending ways of today's seniors. Among the leading alarmists is Peter G. Peterson, the former secretary of commerce and investment banker who recommended austerity for middle-income Americans during the 1980s. He now serves as a spokesman for a group of moderately conservative Republicans and Democrats known as the Concord Coalition. In his influential writings, Peterson has tried to show that American national savings have been decimated by a combination of profligate personal consumption and overreliance on Social Security.[9] By lumping in Medicare and Medicaid deductions, which have skyrocketed because of the lack of a coherent national health plan, Peterson has exaggerated the increase in Social Security deductions. The implication is that the Social Security Administration is mishandling the retirement investments of today's taxpayers.

Nothing could be further from the truth. Social Security is a pay-as-you-go system, in which current payroll deductions support already retired workers. There is no money in retirement accounts. While it is true that in thirty years many more retired people will be reliant on fewer working people, the economy is also expected to grow over that period. The 1996 *Annual Report of the Board of Trustees* (of the Social Security system) predicted that if the economy grows by only 1.8 percent per year until 2030, a lower growth rate than the United States has ever experienced over a long period of time, it will only be necessary to raise deductions slightly, from the current 12.4 percent to 16.4 percent.[10] *Business Week* researched the potential difficulties and reported that "Social Security's financing problems are manageable." One way to change revenues without penalizing the average worker (but probably not what *Business Week* had in mind) would be a progressive expansion of payroll deductions, making them applicable to the highest salaries (deductions in 1996 were limited to incomes up to $61,200).

Some liberals who have bought into the anti–Social Security arguments fear that well-off recipients are draining too much money from programs that could serve others. Lester Thurow, whose economic observations are usually on target, misguidedly attacked Social Security for serving the wealthy: "No public interest is served by making parents rich at the cost of making children poor."[11]

Economist Richard DuBoff countered that Social Security is highly regarded by most Americans precisely because it is a universal program that treats rich and poor alike. Yes, we know that some people who collect Social Security have high incomes—for instance, 3.2 percent of all benefits, about $8 billion, went to those with incomes over $100,000 in 1990—but the solution is to tax them at higher rates for all their income, including investments, rather than penalize them by taking away the small portion of their income that comes from Social Security.

As for conservatives, it is quite possible that another agenda is hidden behind the Social Security scare. If they can dismantle the universality of the program, there will be less public support to sustain it into the future. Proponents of "market-based" retirement solutions hope to convince middle-class and wealthy Americans that their financial security is in doubt, that their investments are imperiled by the high benefits going to lower-middle- and working-class recipients. These critics advocate instead diverting deductions for Social Security into individual retirement accounts, a plan that would undermine the whole system. Opponents of Social Security also say that private pensions will make up for any shortfall in benefits. The truth is that only one retired worker in three currently has a pension, and that it pays on average only $4,500 per year.[12] And of currently employed workers, the percentage who are covered by pension plans has decreased from 50 percent to 44 percent in recent years. It is highly unlikely, given the direction our economy

has been moving for twenty years, that the private sector will devise a way for retirement accounts to benefit the poor and working classes. Pensions, in fact, increasingly benefit those who are already well-off; in just three years, from 1989 to 1992, the share of total pension accounts held by the richest 10 percent of the population increased sharply, from 53 percent to 62 percent.[13]

Privatization of Social Security monies would be dangerous for most Americans because private retirement accounts would not guarantee incomes to the majority of the elderly, who truly need Social Security in order to stay out of poverty. In 1995 the *Social Security Bulletin* noted that without their benefits, two thirds of all elderly would suffer an income drop of 40 percent or more.[14]

Privatization has been pushed by one sector of our society, the small community of investment bankers, who want to tap into this vast vein of unexploited cash. Ideas about the inadequacies of the Social Security system were planted (and then fed and watered) by the investment lobbies in Congress, in particular the Investment Company Institute, which represents the interests of the mutual fund industry. Stock market mutual funds have already come to represent a huge share of American private retirement savings, growing from $716 billion in 1,840 funds in 1986 to more than $3 trillion accumulated in over 7,000 funds by 1996.[15]

In 1995 the mutual fund industry began to set its sights on the extraordinary sums that might be available from Social Security deductions. Lobbyists helped persuade Senator Bob Kerrey of Nebraska to introduce a bill that would allow all workers to direct 2 percent of their wages into their own retirement accounts instead of Social Security. A report generated by a committee at the White House went much further, suggesting that up to 40 percent of the 12.5 percent payroll tax (both employee and employer contributions) could be diverted into "personal security accounts." The result would be "a much bigger windfall for the fund industry—close to $125 billion a year," according to the *New York Times*.[16]

When the stock market is booming, this sounds like a wonderful idea. But at other times—when the market falls, becomes stagnant, or only grows slowly—the risk, especially to lower-income recipients, would become intolerable. Social Security, with its modest administrative costs, provides a much better and more "secure" deal for most retired people.

If the mutual fund companies and their allies keep manufacturing evidence concerning Social Security's coming demise, many people will want to abandon ship. If individuals are allowed to detach themselves from a universal program, it cannot possibly survive its current form. Standards and benefits will erode, leaving lower-income retirees to sink back into poverty. And then, when the stock market finally falls, as it inevitably will, a whole contingent of ex-middle-class escapees from Social Security will be clamoring for help. But at that point, who will be left to guarantee a life-support system for the elderly?

Why Three Deficits?

In this brief review of the "three deficits," it is worth noting that not one of them was caused by "big government." If anything, they resulted from the shortcomings of a weak government that could not stand up to the desires of wealthy investors, financial institutions, and corporations.

1. Robert H. Hayes, "U.S. Competitiveness: 'Resurgence' vs. Reality," *Challenge*, April–May 1996, p. 35.

2. Louis Uchitelle, "Basic Research Is Losing Out," *New York Times*, October 8, 1996, p. A1.

3. Ibid., p. 39.

4. Ibid.

5. Robert Eisner, *The Misunderstood Economy*, Cambridge: The Harvard Business School Press, 1994, and *How Real Is the Federal Deficit?*, New York: Free Press, 1986.

6. David Moberg, "Can the public rescue the infrastructure in a tale of three deficits?" *In These Times*, February 13–19, 1991, based on the work of David Alan Aschauer for the Economic Policy Institute.

7. Richard B. DuBoff, "Government and Social Insurance," *Monthly Review*, October 1995, p. 4.

8. Ibid., p. 7.

9. Peter G. Peterson, *Facing Up*, New York: Simon & Schuster, 1993, and *Will America Grow* *Up Before It Grows Old?*, New York: Random House, 1996. To his credit Peterson did point out that nonpoor Americans received six times as much aid from the government in entitlements as did all of the poor, $680.5 million as opposed to $109.8 million in 1990, and he lamented the fact that we "do next to nothing to help full-time working parents who labor in poverty."

10. DuBoff, "Thurow on Social Security: The 'Left' Strikes Again," *Monthly Review*, October 1996, p. 7.

11. Ibid., p. 8, quoted from Thurow, *The Future of Capitalism*.

12. Ibid., p. 11.

13. Wolff, *Top Heavy*, 1996, p. 64.

14. *The Social Security Bulletin*, Summer 1995, p. 28.

15. Edward Wyatt, "For Mutual Funds, New Political Muscle," *New York Times*, September 8, 1996, pp. F1 and 7.

16. Ibid.

THE MILITARY-INDUSTRIAL COMPLEX AND THE OBSESSION WITH PRIVATIZATION

In the councils of government, we must guard against unwarranted influence, whether sought or unsought, by the military-industrial complex. The potential for the disastrous rise of misplaced power exists and will persist.
—President Dwight D. Eisenhower
in his Farewell Address, 1961

When Eisenhower warned us against the military-industrial complex, he was pointing out that many corporate giants exercised undue influence over our domestic and foreign policies. If the citizenry were not sufficiently aware of these business interests, he cautioned, then the United States could be led in directions that profited the companies at the expense of the common good.

From the end of World War II until the end of the 1980s, the Cold War with the Soviet Union provided the rationale for a massive arms race. A steady and enormous flow of money emanated from the Department of Defense and benefited America's largest industrial corporations. In this process a vast network of lobbying groups and media sources was created to heighten public perception of a Communist military threat. The situation reached its extreme in the early 1980s, when the Reagan administration, calling the Soviet Union the "Evil Empire," pushed military spending rapidly upward, from $118 billion in 1979 to $282 billion in 1987. This provided a bonanza to the military contractors.

PROFIT RATES IN THE DEFENSE INDUSTRY COMPARED WITH OTHER DOMESTIC PRODUCTION[1]		
	1970–79	1980–83
For Department of Defense Hardware	19.4%	23.3%
For Comparable Nondefense Durable Goods	14.4%	10.6%

In the 1970s American corporations were already enjoying higher profits in weapons production than were generally available elsewhere in the economy. But the defense buildup of the early 1980s increased the profit margins even further, to a rate nearly two and a half times greater than similar nonmilitary production.

When the Soviet Union dismantled itself in 1989 and there was no longer a Cold War to justify a huge defense apparatus in the United States, some observers thought the U.S. military-industrial complex would disappear, too. And there were, in fact, some cutbacks in defense spending. The percentage of gross domestic product devoted to the military declined from 6.3 percent at the height of the Reagan buildup to 3.6 percent in the mid-1990s.

But this did not mean that the military-industrial complex had been dismantled. It was merely awaiting the creation of a new threat, which appeared in 1991. In a war that cost very few American lives, the United States punished Iraq for its invasion of Kuwait with one of the fiercest air bombardments in history. Given the public's satisfaction with a "clean" war that seemed like an extension of a child's video game, the defense contractors looked forward to producing a whole new round of sophisticated weapons. Advanced hardware, from "smart bombs" to planes that could fly "blind," won favorable publicity. President Bush claimed that forty-

one of forty-two U.S. Patriot missiles had hit their targets, the more primitive Scud missiles used by Iraq. (The statement later proved to be a gross exaggeration; according to reliable estimates few Patriot missiles ever hit their targets.)[2] Furthermore, a detailed study released by the government in 1996 revealed that high-tech bombs and missiles and the F-117 Stealth fighter plane were not any more effective than the older, far cheaper aircraft and weaponry that previously comprised most of the U.S. arsenal.[3]

This analysis of effectiveness came far too late. Shortly after the Gulf War ended in 1991, the Pentagon announced that it was awarding a new contract to the Lockheed Corporation for the production of an updated Stealth fighter plane that would cost $65 billion. And this was not the only windfall from the war. The recklessness of Saddam Hussein allowed the Pentagon and its allies to begin a campaign to convince the Congress and the American public that a new foreign threat existed. They called it the "rogue state." According to defense analysts, rogue states operated outside the norms of civilized nations and were determined to unleash terror against larger, more pacific countries. One drawback to the theory was that the states in question were generally economic and military weaklings: Cuba, Iraq, North Korea, Iran, and Libya. Their combined military spending amounted to only $9.4 billion in 1995. In comparison, the NATO countries, not counting the United States, spent $147.6 billion on defense, while the U.S. itself was spending $264 billion, 40 percent of the world's total military dollars.[4]

It is unclear whether the rogue state hypothesis was convincing to the general public, but few people protested when the Congress added $11.2 billion on top of President Clinton's requested military budget for

1997. Overall defense spending was staying fairly stable despite steady reductions in the number of armed forces personnel and the continued closings of superfluous military bases. Corporate contractors did not suffer from such cutbacks. The B-2 Stealth bomber, which had never flown in combat and cost more than $2 billion per aircraft, was funded again. The price of a variety of "smart bombs," either already being built or on order, was $58 billion. Secretary of Defense William Perry told contractors that spending on new weapons systems would increase from $38 billion in 1996 to $60 billion per year in 2000.[5] Overall military expenditures in 1997 were maintained at a level that would allow the United States to fight a major war, even though there were no significant military opponents in sight.

In fact, as the twenty-first century begins, the Pentagon continues to argue that it should be able to fight not one, but two major wars in two different parts of the globe at the same time. Retired Air Force Chief of Staff Merrill McPeak gave an honest assessment of this argument: "The two-war strategy is just a marketing device to justify a high budget."[6]

Privatizing War and Privatizing Government

At the time President Eisenhower warned about the influence that the military-industrial complex exerted upon the government, most Americans believed that a massive Cold War defense budget was necessary for national survival. Today it is no longer necessary to marshal this level of public support for government spending, because the process of ceding control of public activities—including the defense of the United States—to private business is much further advanced.

In fact, the nature of corporate interest in defense activities has expanded far beyond the provision of hardware and supplies; today large companies are taking over areas of foreign aid and military support that were once provided by the Department of State or American troops. One company, Military Professional Resources, Inc. (MPRI), which advertises itself as having "The World's Greatest Corporate Military Expertise," has landed big contracts to provide military training to two of the Balkan armies, the Croatian and the Bosnian. Investigative reporter Ken Silverstein found that twenty-two senior corporate officers of MPRI were once senior military officers in the U.S. Armed Forces, including retired general Carl Vuono, who was U.S. Army Chief of Staff in the early 1990s. MPRI is being paid $400 million to train the Bosnian Army but most of the money comes neither from the United States nor from Bosnia itself; instead it is supplied by countries such as Saudi Arabia, Kuwait, Brunei, and Malaysia.[7]

In June of 1997, the Defense Intelligence Agency (or D.I.A., a part of the Department of Defense) invited potential corporate contractors to a closed-door symposium on "The Privatization of National-Security Functions in Sub-Saharan Africa."[8] In effect, the D.I.A. was promoting a growth industry; the increasing use of mercenary forces to support or topple the governments of African nations has opened new opportunities for American companies and unemployed ex-military personnel. Such efforts can threaten the development of democracy in other countries, but they also pose a danger to democratic decision-making in the United States. Privately run military operations can either circumvent the intentions of our government or they can be used clandestinely by the Defense Department, the Department of State, or the CIA (à la Oliver North's

Iran-*contra* operation of the 1980s) in order to keep unseemly strategies out of the public eye.

The privatization of military activity raises an even larger issue about how democracies function and who is responsible for public policy. "Market solutions" utilizing private enterprise are now applied to many areas—prisons, police departments, hospitals, welfare systems, and schools—that were formerly handled by local, state, and federal governments or by nonprofit corporations that were subject to public oversight. In some cases, private business arrived on the scene at a time when local and state governments were so financially strapped by budget cuts that they could not afford to carry out their duties, much less invest in modernizing technology. At other times, a political choice to "reduce the size of government" led to immediate openings for private operations to take over.

The Welfare Reform Act of 1996, for example, slashed benefits for the poor, but allowed private companies to line up for their share of the support checks. Because the Welfare Reform Act designated that states would receive lump-sum payments for welfare programs that previously had been handled by the federal government, states suddenly had tens of billions of dollars that they had to process and disburse to individuals each year. A number of states sought to contract out the work to private businesses, such as Lockheed Information Services (a subsidiary of the giant defense contractor Lockheed Martin). In a bidding war in Texas, the object was to take over $563 million in state welfare operations; among the bidders was Electronic Data Systems, the outfit that once made a huge fortune for Ross Perot by handling computerized records of Medicare and Social Security disbursements. Another

contractor, a $4.2 billion subsidiary of the giant accounting firm Arthur Anderson, warned of the possible boondoggles: "There's some easy money if the states aren't careful."

These cautionary words involved more than competition for a big contract. Abuse of the system had occurred before when Lockheed Information Services was banned from New York City for its part in a political influence-peddling scandal that involved parking meter collections. Electronic Data Systems was called "grossly inefficient" by the attorney general of Florida due to the way it handled a large welfare contract in that state.[9]

Lockheed Martin was so intent on entering the welfare market that it hired a new senior vice president, Gerald Miller, who had previously been employed by the state of Michigan to direct the dismantling of social programs. If there was any doubt about what was motivating "welfare reform," Miller cleared it up: "The private sector will ultimately run these programs. The era of big government is over."[10] He might have added that the era of big business running big government was well under way. Later in the same month, September 1996, Lockheed Martin was still expanding operations in its old line of work, aerospace. It signed a $7 billion contract to take over part of the space shuttle program for NASA.

Can everything be privatized? At first glance, some public ventures do not seem to lend themselves to colonization by giant corporations. One of these is public education, an area of American life where the tradition of direct community control through democratically elected school boards is well established. However, when the new breed of corporate investors looks at the nation's public school systems, they see something else: the possibility of taking over a giant economic entity that generates six hundred billion dollars in revenue each year. The prospects are indeed bright for the development of a new "education market." In 1996 the Lehman Brothers investment firm sponsored "the first educational investment conference"; their managing director foresaw a rosy future for "a local industry that over time will become a global business."[11]

1. From a study for the Pentagon cited in *The 1987 Defense Budget*, by Joshua M. Epstein, Washington: The Brookings Institute, 1987.

2. " 'Smart' Weapons Were Overrated by Pentagon," *New York Times*, July 6, 1996, p. A1.

3. Ibid.

4. Seymour Melman, *New York Times*, June 26, 1995.

5. William D. Hartung, "Pumping Up the Pentagon," *Dollars and Sense*, May–June 1996, p. 37.

6. Ibid.

7. Ken Silverstein, "Privatizing War," *The Nation*, July 28/August 4, 1997, pp. 11–17.

8. Ibid.

9. Nina Bernstein, "Giant Companies Entering Race to Run State Welfare Programs," *New York Times*, September 15, 1996, p. A1.

10. Russell Baker, "Except for the Pentagon," *New York Times*, September 24, 1996, p. A25.

11. Phyllis Vine, "To Market, to Market: The School Business Sells Kids Short," *The Nation*, September 8–15, 1997, p. 11.

WHEELING AND DEALING, GAMBLING AND STEALING

With adequate profit, capital is very bold. A certain 10 percent will ensure its employment elsewhere; 20 percent will produce eagerness; 50 percent audacity; 100 percent will make it ready to trample on all human laws; 300 percent, and there is not a crime which it will not scruple, nor a risk it will not run, even to the chance of its owner being hanged.

—KARL MARX

In many ways the American economy has become a high-stakes game where the players take big risks on making incredible returns. In the 1980s, according to a cover story in *Business Week*, the United States turned into a "Casino Society." This was the same label that economist John Maynard Keynes applied to the business world of the 1920s, when the interests of the financial economy far outweighed those of the productive economy. Keynes also warned, "Speculators may do no harm as a bubble on a steady stream of enterprise. But the position becomes serious when enterprise becomes a bubble on a whirlpool of speculation."

Government deregulation in the past two decades has encouraged three kinds of high-risk activity. The first is the traditional kind of gambling. Many states have legalized the construction of gaudy casinos where many working people, no longer able to bet that hard work will pay off in increased wages, are putting their faith in the slot machines instead. Meanwhile many other middle-class and upper-class Americans are playing another, much grander game in the stock market. Their goals are more or less the same as the small-time casino gamblers. They hope that their money, without any effort or labor on their own part, will miraculously multiply. They dream of being super-investors like Warren Buffet, who plunked his money down on some popular numbers and walked away billions richer in 1997 than he had been in 1995.

A third kind of gambling, which requires more calculation, involves those who bet that they can push the limits of fraud and corruption without getting caught. The people who are supposed to be guiding the engines of modern capital—bankers and corporate directors and government representatives—have gone on a rampage of speculation and theft that has wasted or destroyed trillions of dollars in assets.

The Great Savings and Loan Robbery—$500 Billion Gone

During the 1980s, the banking system of the United States was looted and nearly collapsed. It was not until the end of the decade that the public began to be informed of the magnitude of the mismanagement and fraud in the savings and loan industry. Theft from the public treasury—in the form of taxpayer-subsidized reimbursements for S&L depositors' losses—surpassed $500 billion.[1] This should be compared to the record of bank robbers, who were clearly not operating in the same league: the losses from all armed robberies of U.S. banks in 1987 only amounted to $37 million.[2]

Along with other financial businesses, the savings and loan industry was deregulated in the late 1970s and early 1980s. The story of its undoing during the Reagan administration bears retelling.

Savings and loan institutions had originally been created as a vehicle for providing working- and middle-class citizens with a steady source of mortgage money to purchase homes. But in 1981, Richard Pratt, a finance professor from the University of Utah, was selected as chairman of the Federal Home Loan Bank Board. A fanatic on the "free market" and deregulation of financial institutions, Pratt eased the rules for savings and loans: bank examinations were no longer stringent or frequent; and owners were required to have less capital than formerly to back up their loans and operations. An important rule that S&Ls have at least four hundred stockholders (formerly considered a proof of their community involvement) was dropped; and the S&Ls were actually prodded to give up the time-honored practice of providing mortgages to individual home owners in order to pursue the much more lucrative business of lending to commercial real estate developers.[3] Many of these were poorly secured, high-interest loans to shopping-mall and luxury apartment projects; the S&Ls also made big investments in the high-yielding, high-risk "junk bond" market. The change was dramatic:

PERCENTAGE OF S&L LOANS GOING TO HOME MORTGAGES	
1981	1987
65%	39%

One of the architects of banking deregulation was Republican Senator Jake Garn of Utah, who loaned his name to the main piece of banking legislation: the Garn–St. Germain Depository Institutions Act. For his efforts, Garn was enshrined in history at the University of Utah when the Garn Institute of Finance was established in his honor. The major donors behind the institute were large savings and loan institutions which had been speculating in high-risk junk bonds, and Drexel Burnham Lambert, the Wall Street firm that specialized in marketing such "junk." Garn received more speaking fees from the S&L industry than any other senator of his time. Senator Garn's chief aide in charge of banking matters, M. Danny Wall, was selected by Ronald Reagan as the chairman of the Federal Home Loan Bank Board in 1987.[4]

Politicians of both parties were easily persuaded to look the other way. Democratic Senators Alan Cranston of California, Dennis DeConcini of Arizona, Timothy Wirth of Colorado, and Donald Riegle of Michigan, along with Republican John McCain of Arizona, were duped by banker Charles Keating, who orchestrated one of the largest S&L frauds in history. Keating funneled $1.3 million into their election campaigns in hopes of receiving preferential treatment from the Senate Banking Committee. In the House, Jim Wright, the Democratic Speaker, received personal gifts amounting to nearly $100,000 from friends in the savings and loan industry in Texas. When the graft was revealed, Wright was forced to resign.

Many private citizens were luckier. For instance, Neil Bush, son of President Bush, was a member of the board of directors of Silverado Savings and Loan in Colorado. He and his fellow board members made substantial loans to their own friends and business associates. But these loans were often unsecured; that is, the borrowers were not obliged to put up collateral to be used to repay the loans. Silverado, like so many other savings and loans, collapsed because of these unsound dealings. Documents prepared by the Office of Thrift Supervision in 1990 were quite revealing; for example, a loss of $45 million resulted from unsecured loans to a single individual, William L. Walters, who was a business associate of Neil Bush. The total cost to taxpayers for the Silverado bailout was approximately $1 billion. (Neither Bush nor his friends were charged with a crime, but thirteen of them did agree to pay $49.5 million in damages to the Federal Deposit Insurance Corporation. Of that total, $26.5 million was covered by their liability insurance and the other $23 million came from a legal defense fund which Silverado had prudently amassed during its heyday.)

Who gained from these fiascos? First, there were the bank officers, board members, and their friends who borrowed large sums of unsecured money and were under little legal obligation to pay the money back. The Federal Home Loan Bank Board found evidence of fraud and other criminal activity by managers and directors at 75 percent of the failing S&Ls, but prosecuted very few of them.[5] Secondly, big depositors, who were lured to obscure S&Ls by promises of the highest interest rates in the land, gained because their $100,000 certificates of deposit were fully insured by the government. Finally, financial brokers did well; each time they moved money for large depositors—often they found the highest returns for investors in the Northeast in the fledgling institutions of the Southwest—they collected a fee.

The thousands of financiers, lawyers, and politicians who participated in the debacle thought they were just "playing the game." In such circumstances, Bill and Hillary Clinton were by no means unusual, except that for them the gamble did not pay off; their ill-advised involvement with a troubled S&L, Madison Guaranty Trust, continues to haunt them to this day. The Clintons were persuaded to participate in Madison

Guaranty's investments by their friends Jim and Susan McDougal; when they saw their savings begin to disappear, they decided to cut their losses. The McDougals, as principal owners of the little S&L, were more unlucky; after it failed, they were convicted of fraud.

Here the Bucks Never Stop

It is worth noting that the losses of the S&Ls were not an anomaly. At the same time they went down in flames, burning up half a trillion dollars, the nation's largest commercial banks were losing over a trillion dollars, mostly from extreme overinvestment in the development and construction of big office buildings. Corporate giants such as Citibank were rescued from failure in 1990 only because the Federal Reserve Board and wealthy foreign investors infused huge sums of cash in the commercial banking system. What encouraged such ill-advised risk-taking at the expense of investment in productive enterprises?

First of all, the "financialization" of business was taking place. The Finance, Insurance, and Real Estate (FIRE) sector of the economy, which thrives on the making of quick deals, had grown to be immense, by some measures larger than the manufacturing sector or the service sector. Secondly, the concentration on financial activities and the rapid computerization of all business transactions led to a rather peculiar boom in financial "inventions." Human ingenuity that had once created a wealth of new machinery and service processes was channeled into ways to make money travel more quickly and smoothly around the globe. Electronic manipulation of money transactions, currency exchanges, and commodity futures grew so huge that microscopic distor-

tions in value on the computer screen could translate into millions of dollars in profit to the alert trader. New financial instruments, known as derivatives, multiplied rapidly: T-Bill and T-bond futures appeared in the 1970s; "swaptions" and "options," Euro futures and captions came on in the 1980s; SLOBs and SURFs (Sale-Leaseback Obligation Bonds and Step-Up Recovery Floaters) were on-line in the 1990s.

The exotic-sounding names of derivatives suggest the obscurity of the newest financial markets, where speculators could go way beyond the "margins" allowed in the stock market and earn incredible returns if they bet correctly. Buyers could see their derivatives rising or falling—but in relation to what? Often their wagers were connected to no real economic activity. This financial economy overshadowed the so-called real economy; it processed $800 billion every day in the early 1990s, forty times as much as the $20 billion exchange daily in the global trade of the real economy.

Finance was also getting the upper hand within big industrial corporations. General Electric gave up the production of consumer electronic goods altogether and concentrated instead on financial speculation through subsidiaries such as General Electric Credit. The financial arms of Ford and General Motors (Ford Credit Corporation and GMAC, respectively) became more profitable than the manufacturing operations themselves. The financial services empire at Ford was so successful that it accounted for three fifths of company earnings in 1993; and in the third quarter of 1996, it garnered 98 percent of the company's profits, or $671 million. Its most successful subsidiary was the Ford Credit Corporation, which controlled consumer loans at dealerships all over the country and, like GMAC, earned the reputation of bilking low-income buyers who could not get other kinds of credit.[6]

Other strong profit-makers for Ford were the subsidiaries Associates Corporation of America and First Family Financial Services, which went after lower-income, less sophisticated buyers of used autos and homes, hitting them with exorbitant interest rates and manipulative terms. A new division, called Fairlane, opened in December of 1996 with the express purpose of going after bad credit risks and charging usurious rates of 18 percent to 22 percent and up. One former loan officer and assistant manager of Associates Corporation in Alabama described the company attitude about running up the cost of broker fees and finance points: "If you had to lie about points that we charged, lie to 'em. They're stupid anyway."[7]

Taking Risks and Making Theft Acceptable

This kind of behavior—treating each customer like a sucker to be milked for all he's worth—once existed only on the fringes of business, among loan sharks, bookies, and peddlers of dubious get-rich-quick deals. In the 1980s the rip-off artists were operating in the mainstream. A few, like money managers Michael Milken and Ivan Boesky, used the promise of ultrahigh returns to fool rich private investors into forking over huge sums for junk bonds and other derivatives.

By the 1990s public officials, supposedly charged with protecting taxpayers' billions of dollars in assets, were being suckered into similar games. In one of the most egregious examples, the treasurer of Orange County, California, Robert L. Citron, was lured into investing $21 billion in financial derivatives, thinking that the earnings would lower the taxes of his constituents. He then arranged

for the county to create and sell its own bonds to investors, who were unaware that the county was overextended in the derivative market. When the market collapsed, Orange County declared bankruptcy rather than face its financial obligations to the bondholders.

If the Orange County treasurer was extraordinarily stupid in his attempts to break into the world of high finance, he was not the major villain in the story. Merrill Lynch, the nation's largest securities firm, had enticed him into the deal. It earned huge fees by selling the county two thirds of its $21 billion in securities, then turned around and underwrote $875 million in the worthless bonds that the county issued. In 1996 the Securities and Exchange Commission announced its intentions to charge Merrill Lynch with fraud as an underwriter, a year after Orange County had filed suit against the firm for its failings as a broker.[8]

Milken, Boesky, and Citron were all convicted of crimes, but that was unusual. A general shift in business culture had persuaded all kinds of employees, not just a few high-flying entrepreneurs, to risk going outside the boundaries of fair play. They were encouraged to use devious and fraudulent selling methods, and they seldom got caught or punished. Such practices, deemed acceptable because they produced higher corporate profits and bonuses for the individuals involved, pervaded the internal "cultures" of many corporations. Prudential, the nation's number one insurance company, is one example.

From the mid-1980s to the mid-1990s Prudential permitted its agents to encourage millions of customers to cash in or borrow against existing insurance policies and buy new ones. The agents did this without informing the customers that the new policies offered less coverage at a higher cost.

When finally threatened with prosecution by the Justice Department in 1996, Prudential agreed to a settlement of $410 million in an attempt to compensate the 10.7 million customers who might have been cheated during this period. But many state insurance commissioners were not satisfied, for lawsuits they had filed against Prudential required settlements well beyond the $410 million. Prudential was not alone in its skullduggery. In the few years before Prudential's settlement, other giant insurance companies—such as John Hancock Mutual Life, Metropolitan Life, and New York Life—were forced to make similar restitution to customers they had bilked. According to the *New York Times*, "These cases have embarrassed the industry, and, many executives say, contributed to a decline in sales."[9]

In the meantime, Prudential and the other insurance giants had also become diversified companies that dealt in real estate sales and stocks and bonds and derivatives. Just as insurance fraud was proceeding in one part of the corporation, Prudential's securities-brokerage unit was being forced to pay $1.5 billion to aggrieved customers who had been enticed into buying shares in shaky limited partnerships. These shares were not the "safe" investments advertised by the Prudential salespeople; they were, in effect, very risky gambles on personal savings, and the customers had lost their shirts.

Gambling and Dealing

At one time, large-scale gambling activity in the United States was considered illegal everywhere but in the remote deserts of Nevada. Now a majority of states are engaged in an immense enterprise, both private and public, to promote gambling as a wholesome family activity. Today, gambling is no longer a small-time player on the periphery, but a mainstream "industry" that capitalizes on a growing addiction: Americans' gambling losses amount to $40 to $50 billion per year.[10]

States and localities became infatuated with gambling when federal revenue sharing started to dry up in the 1980s. State governments created lotteries—under the banner of financing schools or programs for the elderly—instead of raising taxes. Like sales taxes, lotteries are regressive and take more money out of the pockets of the poor and the working classes than from the well-to-do. And like slot machines in the casinos, state-sponsored lotteries offer very low chances of winning. The gambling casino corporations smelled an opportunity and explained to both state governors and Native American tribes how they could share in the action. New betting emporiums were allowed to spring up in waterfront resort areas and on reservation lands, and state and local governments profited from the highly lucrative and regressive tax that was tacked onto the revenues of the casinos.

How did gambling get so popular? Corporations recognized the potential for annual profit rates of 30 percent to 50 percent, at least twice those of other high-return businesses. Las Vegas casino owners began to flex their newfound political muscle. They created the American Gaming Association, headed by lawyer Frank Fahrenkopf (who earned $800,000 per year and was the former chairman of the Republican National Committee). Before the 1996 elections, gambling kingpin Steve Wynn had raised over a million dollars for the Republican National Committee, then realized he ought to play it safe by covering both horses. So, in June of 1996, at an event organized by Wynn, rich residents of Las Vegas paid $25,000 per couple to eat lunch with President Clinton, raising $650,000 for the Democrats at a single stroke.

But Republicans were not to be outdone. After Newt Gingrich ate dinner with Wynn in Las Vegas, the Speaker told local Republicans they should not worry about a federal gaming commission that was being set up by the Congress; any study of gambling, he said, would be structured "so that the commission does not have the power to issue subpoenas." Meanwhile Bill Clinton played golf on Wynn's private course, collected the Democrats' lunch money, and told Las Vegans that he now opposed a proposal, generated in the White House two years earlier, to slap a 4 percent federal tax on casino revenues. "That was never a recommendation of my cabinet," Clinton explained, "much less of anyone in the White House."[11]

1. Robert Kuttner, *Everything for Sale*, New York: Knopf, 1996, p. 174. Based on Congressional Budget Office figures that include the immediate cost of the bailout, $160 billion to $200 billion, plus the interest payments that would be incurred by taxpayers through the year 2000.

2. Statement by FBI chief William Sessions, 1989.

3. David Maranias and Rick Atkinson, "The Texas S&L Meltdown," *Washington Post Weekly Edition*, June 26–July 2, 1989; Kathleen Day, "A Lobby's Decline and Fall: Bailout Erodes S&L Industry's Clout," *Washington Post*, July 28, 1989.

4. Ibid.

5. Editorial, *Washington Post Weekly Edition*, July 10–16, 1989.

6. For descriptions of just how widespread such corporate practice is, see Michael Hudson, ed., *Merchants of Misery*, Monroe, ME: Common Courage Press, 1996.

7. Michael Hudson, "Cashing in on Poverty," *The Nation*, May 20, 1996, p. 12.

8. "SEC Is Said to Plan Fraud Case Against Merrill Lynch," *New York Times*, September 20, 1996, p. D2.

9. Joseph B. Treaster, "Prudential to Pay Policyholders $410 Million for Its Sales Tactics," *New York Times*, October 12, 1996, pp. D1 and D3.

10. Sally Denton and Roger Morris, "Easy Money in Vegas," *New York Times*, July 9, 1996, p. A19.

11. Ibid.

ONE-PARTY POLITICS:
THE VICTORY OF
THE MONEY PARTY

When the public discovers that its only choice is between Republicans and Republicans who call themselves Democrats, between those who champion the rich without qualms and those who champion the rich with an echo of regret, they'll opt for the real thing.

—ROBERT REICH, Democratic campaign consultant,
commenting on Michael Dukakis's
presidential defeat in 1988

I think the Dukakis campaign badly miscalculated thinking that they could get away with an issueless campaign. I'm very glad they did not develop the populist theme that they [belatedly began] in the last two weeks . . . There is constantly a war going on between the two parties for the populist vote, the swing vote in every election. The Democrats have always got to nail the Republicans as the party of the fat cats, the party of upper class and privilege. And the Democrats will maintain that they're the party of the common man.

—LEE ATWATER, Republican campaign manager
for George Bush in 1988

n the 1988 presidential campaign, the Democratic Party chose to blur the distinction between itself and the Republicans, a strategy that played right into the hands of the GOP. Later, in spite of Clinton's victories in the 1992 and 1996 elections, the Democrats never dared to launch a populist attack on the "fat cats" and to hold them responsible for the economic inequality created in the 1980s. This reluctance can be explained by the Democrats' unwillingness to criticize the sources of their funds, which increasingly come from corporate Political Action Committees (PACs), as well as wealthy patrons.

As a consequence, we now have a political environment in which Democrats and Republicans act as two wings of one big party—the Money Party. In the process they have lost the trust of the American people. Most citizens no longer feel that they are participating in a democracy. This was not always the case.

HOW AMERICANS VIEWED THEIR GOVERNMENT, 1960 AND 1994
"The government is pretty much run by a few big interests looking out for themselves."[1]
Percentage Who Agree: 1960—30%   1994—79%
"The government is run for the benefit of all."
Percentage Who Agree: 1960—65%   1994—15%

As the century draws to a close, more and more Americans feel that our political system is incapable of responding to our social and economic problems. Why, we ask ourselves, is it so difficult to change course? Are we really too powerless and demoralized to take political action?

No, but in order to do so effectively we must examine the links between various social, cultural, and political forces and the economic prerogatives of the few. Although some of these forces seem archaic—like the class structure—they are constantly adapted to serve the changing needs of corporations and wealthy individuals. In the following three chapters, we will briefly explore the ways such forces limit the range of political discourse, promote upper-class dominance, and drive an increasing number of Americans to accept authoritarian solutions to social and economic problems.

The Money Party

The public perception that "the government is pretty much run by a few big interests looking out for themselves" is an accurate one. During the 1996 election campaigns, the Democrats and Republicans simply auctioned off their national conventions to the highest bidders. By selling corporate sponsorships, and by allowing companies to provide for all the needs of delegates with donated products, the parties changed the very nature of what happens at a political convention. For instance, Richard C. Notebaert, CEO of the Ameritech Corporation and a registered Republican, was an "honorary chairman" at the Democratic convention in Chicago. When a reporter asked him what he was doing there he pointed to an advertisement of a Democratic donkey talking on a telephone and said, "This is what it's all about." His company, a $13-billion-a-year telecommunications firm, was the single largest donor to the convention, supplying a huge state-of-the-art cellular communications system for the use of all the delegates and reporters. Ameritech's contribution, which won it the designation as "Official Communications Company" of the Democratic convention, was not unusual; the heads of seventy-two other corporations that gave at least $100,000 to the Democrats each earned the title of "Honorary Chairman of the Convention."[2]

This kind of corporate sponsorship brings a double benefit. Like conventional political donations, it buys loyalty from politicians. For instance, an Anheuser-Busch vice president at the Democratic convention frankly admitted that his company was hoping the federal government would lower its tax on beer. The corporate presence also serves as a form of advertisement. At the Republican convention in San Diego, whose costs were auctioned off to corporate bidders in exactly the same way, another telecommunications giant, Pacific Telesis, provided visitors with its latest cellular phones. A company spokesman said, "We were pleased. We showcased our technology in a highly visible place."[3]

They Get What They Pay For

What was startling in the 1996 elections was the equality of corporate treatment; Republicans no longer had a lopsided advantage over the Democrats. Not only were the business donations to the two conventions more balanced, but the donations of PACs and rich individuals to the parties' campaign funds were becoming more equally divided, too.

The total amount expended represented an extraordinary increase in the power of financial interests to control elections. The $800 million spent on the presidential race was three times higher than in 1992. A similar amount was spent on the congressional elections.[4] With indirect spending thrown in, the total expense of the 1996 elections went well over $2 billion. At that rate, the $74 million that went to each party from federal election funds—mandated by Congress in the 1970s

in order to offset the contributions of the wealthy and powerful—was a pittance. The most important growth in funding came in the form of "soft money," the unrestricted contributions made to the parties themselves rather than to individual candidates. Republicans still had an edge in this category by November of 1996, taking in $274 million to the Democrats' $195 million.[5]

But Democratic fund-raisers were happy. For more than two decades a much larger share of this money, as well as PAC contributions, had been going to the Republicans, who were clearly definable as the party of business and the well-to-do.[6] This had not always been so. From the 1930s through the 1960s, campaign spending had been lower, and roughly equal amounts were raised by Republicans and Democrats; the latter received a large proportion of their funds from labor unions.

Equity in fund-raising began to change in 1968 when presidential candidate Richard Nixon, by using some unusual arm-twisting on wealthy political friends, demonstrated that Republicans could raise twice as much money as Hubert Humphrey and the Democrats. The 1971 Federal Election Campaign Act was supposed to stem the flood of money from rich individual donors. But it also gave birth to the financing creatures known as PACs. Labor and business PACs contributed roughly equal amounts in the 1972 elections, but corporate PACs soon took the lead. By 1980 business was outspending labor by a margin of 3 to 1; in 1984 it upped the margin to 4 to 1; by the end of the 1980s, according to political scientists Joel Rogers and Thomas Ferguson, business had cranked up the advantage to 7 to 1.[7] The same ratio was maintained in 1996, in spite of a special election drive staged by the AFL-CIO.[8]

Because of this overwhelming advantage, the Democratic Party's national ticket began to sidestep associations with organized labor (while still accepting its donations, of course). Instead, the party courted big business. A detailed analysis of all "soft money" contributions in 1992 showed that members of the Finance, Insurance, and Real Estate (FIRE) sector gave lavishly to both parties, helping the Democrats narrow the overall Republican fund-raising advantage in "soft money" to less than 2 to 1. In the "hard money" competition, where industry PACs gave directly to campaigns, the FIRE sector was again the biggest donor, with $29 million, and for the first time more than half of its money went to the Democratic Party.[9]

Had the Democrats become the party of Wall Street? Not exactly, but they had managed to become the slightly poorer wing of the Money Party. The Clinton administration appointed Robert Rubin of Goldman Sachs to head the National Economic Council and then made him the secretary of the treasury, where he turned into the most influential of all Clinton's cabinet members. Rubin had shown his value in 1984, when he raised $1.8 million for the Democrats (a big sum in those days) at a time when most of the investment community supported Ronald Reagan.

The Significance of Bill Clinton

When in 1996 the *Wall Street Journal* concluded that Bill Clinton was running the "most conservative Democratic campaign since Grover Cleveland," it suggested an interesting parallel with the situation that existed a century earlier.

Democratic President Grover Cleveland had pursued a fairly conservative course in the early 1890s, generally favoring the business interests of the Robber Barons who dominated the era. But in 1894 he made the mistake of signing a bill, pushed by the populists in his party, that instituted a federal income tax. For this the Democrats were severely punished in 1896. Political strategist Mark Hanna raised so much money from the upper class, the owners of the trusts and monopolies, that Republicans outspent Democrats by a margin of 10 to 1. This proved enough to defeat the popular William Jennings Bryan at the polls, and the age of modern business politics was born. J. P. Morgan and John D. Rockefeller each gave $250,000 to the Republican Party, an enormous sum in those days; together they had nearly matched the entire Democratic campaign fund of $600,000.

One hundred years later Bill Clinton might have remembered the fate of Grover Cleveland when the Republicans dominated the 1994 congressional elections. The GOP took control of the House of Representatives because monied interests and upper-income voters were extremely displeased with the modest income tax increases enacted by Democrats in 1993. Clinton, with his nimble political instincts, moved quickly to the right, won the 1996 election, and in the process abandoned any loyalty to the old populist core values of his party. Clinton recaptured the presidency and conservative Republicans solidified their control of the Senate and House. No matter which party claimed the victory, money had triumphed.

Although many liberals felt that they had been suddenly betrayed by Clinton, his loyalties had always been suspect, a fact reflected in his previous political and social connections. In 1985 Clinton had helped found the Democratic Leadership Council (DLC), a group that depended on corporate sponsorship and had very few ties to organized labor. Its mission was to shed the liberal label associated with the party. Moderate southern Democrats, who had lost ground to the GOP in the late 1970s and early 1980s, were attracted to the Republican values embodied in the DLC. The DLC wanted to assist corporate expansion by supporting cutbacks in the size of government. It also wanted to convince the elite, both the old-money donors and the new entrepreneurs, that dynamic Sun Belt leaders like Bill Clinton could do business with them.

Arkansas as a Developing Country— Hustling the New Elites

In the conservative atmosphere that prevailed in the 1980s, the governors of the Sun Belt states had shepherded nonunionized workforces into new industrial plants built by domestic and foreign corporations. The sales pitch to the transnational companies was simple: low wages, low taxes, and no organized labor.

Within the United States it is impossible to find a poorer, less developed place than Arkansas, not even by crossing the river into Mississippi; its levels of income, education, and other social indicators all hover around forty-ninth and fiftieth place on the list of the fifty states. In spite of this (or because of it), Arkansas was home to a number of booming industries during Bill Clinton's tenure as governor. Three companies in particular gained national prominence by exploiting their principal advantage—poorly paid workers—in order to increase their market share.

First, there is Wal-Mart, the preeminent discount retailer in the country. It employs over six hundred thousand people, almost as many as Manpower or General Motors. Wal-Mart is expert in taking advantage of marginalized workers and women entering the labor force; it also epitomizes the ability of large corporate interests to overwhelm the small retailers of Main Street, USA. Wal-Mart has become a highly efficient marketer of cheap clothing manufactured by the poorest industrial workers in the world, whether they work in Asia, Africa, or Latin America. As a sideline Wal-Mart owns the second-largest chain of supermarkets in the country. The five members of the Walton family (the wife and four children of the deceased founder) possessed the second-largest fortune in the United States, valued at $23.6 billion in 1996.

Another, less famous Arkansas-based company is the Beverly Nursing Home chain, owner of hundreds of for-profit facilities for the elderly all over the United States. Beverly has cashed in on the biggest revenue stream, older people, within the biggest service industry, health care. The company is infamous for its mistreatment of workers: it holds down wages, increases workloads and patient-to-employee ratios, and decreases the number of higher-paid, more highly trained registered nurses. Beverly's rough tactics give it an advantage over smaller nursing home chains (many of which it has acquired or put out of business), and it has been cited for hundreds of labor law violations in its battles to keep its employees from joining unions.

A third Arkansas giant is Tyson Foods, the world's largest producer of chickens. Tyson depends on low-cost rural labor to grow its chickens on factory-farms and to butcher and package them in seventy-eight processing plants. Its high profitability is based on the fast-paced and dangerous production lines that typify the meatpacking industry. Tyson's food operations also involve other agricultural commodities. The principal owner, Donald John Tyson, is worth $950 million and has been a big-money Clinton backer for years.[10]

Such corporations found it expedient to have a reliable financier right at home in Arkansas. The Stephens investment conglomerate grew immense—*Forbes* magazine called it the largest financial firm in the country outside of New York—by underwriting the expansion of Wal-Mart and financing new divisions of Tyson Foods. Jack Stephens, the principal owner, also became a billionaire and a contributor to the political success of Bill Clinton.

These kinds of businesses, which developed in advance of Bill Clinton's career, helped form the Arkansas milieu in which the president-to-be (and his wife) learned about economic life in America and made the connections that are the prerequisites for political success. Hillary Rodham Clinton worked for the most prestigious law firm in the state, the Rose Law Firm, which Bill Clinton's biographer David Maraniss called "the legal arm of the powerful, representing, among others, the holy trinity of Arkansas business and industry: Stephens, Inc., Tyson Foods, and Wal-Mart."[11] Sometimes the connections resulted in a nicely timed personal favor, as when Hillary Clinton made her famous shrewd investment in commodities futures. She netted $100,000 on a $1,000 cash advance by following the explicit advice of the chief legal counsel at Tyson Foods, Jim Blair.

At other times, the stakes were far higher. A brief recounting of the most publicized political scandal of 1996 will illustrate just how incestuous and inbred politics and business in Arkansas had become.

Years ago, Arkansas financier Jack Stephens befriended Mochtar Riady, a wealthy Indo-

nesian banker. In 1977 Stephens arranged to train Riady's twenty-year-old son, James, as an intern in his bank in Little Rock. James stayed on in Arkansas, according to the *Wall Street Journal*, to "socialize with Little Rock's corporate gentry," and became a good friend of Bill Clinton's. By the age of twenty-eight Riady was president of the Worthen Bank, which the Riady family owned jointly with Stephens, and he was up to his eyeballs in the kinds of fraudulent financial operations that typified the 1980s. Joe Giroir, the managing partner in the Rose Law Firm, had prepared much of the paperwork for the Worthen Bank as well as concocting the biggest S&L boondoggle in Arkansas at an institution call First-South. When FirstSouth's failure, which cost taxpayers $600 million, was examined by federal banking agents, the Rose Law Firm had to pay Federal regulators a settlement of $3 million to avoid a lawsuit involving Giroir's conduct. Giroir was forced to leave Rose Law, but he continued to represent the Stephens empire and the Riady family interests.[12]

Years later, in the fall of 1996, Clinton was sailing comfortably toward victory in the presidential election, riding a wave of business support no Democrat had enjoyed for decades. Then, in mid-October, a potentially damaging story appeared, revealing that U.S. capitalists were not the only enthusiasts for the Clinton campaign. It seemed that John Huang, once employed at the Department of Commerce, had joined the Democratic National Committee (DNC) in order to drum up $4 million to $5 million in campaign contributions from Asian-Americans. In the process he also dealt surreptitiously with the Lippo company, a $12 billion Indonesian conglomerate owned by none other than the Riady family. Huang arranged for the Riadys to make illegal contributions of $250,000 through one of their subsidiary companies in South Korea and another $425,000 from Indonesians who were temporarily living in Washington.

The most interesting revelation was the fact that John Huang had once worked directly with James Riady, the heir to the Lippo empire and the same young man who had been sponsored by Governor Clinton of Arkansas as a banking intern in 1977. Huang, as the executive in charge of Lippo operations in the United States, had helped Riady pave the way for joint ventures between Lippo companies and American banks and insurance companies in Asia. Huang received $700,000 in severence pay from Lippo in 1994, when he left to take a job at the Commerce Department, a position he held until he moved to the DNC.

Joe Giroir, Hillary Clinton's old boss at Rose Law, was now an international deal-maker who specialized in Arkansas-Indonesian-Chinese connections; he negotiated various projects on behalf of the Lippo Co., including the opening of the first giant Wal-Mart store in Jakarta and the construction of a billion-dollar power plant in China. Huang, Riady, and Giroir remained in constant contact; their most famous reunion took place in the Oval Office of the White House in September of 1995, when the three of them met with President Clinton.[13]

We still don't know exactly what was promised in this meeting, but we should not imagine that the globalization of American political fund-raising was limited to the Democrats. Republicans have been equally adept at tapping into foreign funds for their campaigns. Testifying before a Senate committee in 1997, Republican Party Chairman Haley Barbour had to reveal his own embarrassing Asian connection with a bevy of bankers from Hong Kong. Regardless of the source of the money, however, it has become clear that all American political fund-raising has been corrupted by the more or less legal influence of big money.

1. *New York Times*, November 6, 1996, p. B13.

2. Leslie Wayne, "Convention Was Brought to You By . . .", *New York Times*, September 1, 1996, p. 36.

3. Ibid.

4. Leslie Wayne, " 'Soft Money' Far Outpaces Other Gifts, U.S. Reports," *New York Times*, October 25, 1996, p. A28; "Money Votes," *The Nation*, November 11, 1996, p. 5.

5. *Washington Post*, November 3, 1996. Figures through the month of September 1996.

6. Ruth Marcus and Charles B. Babcock, "Record Amounts of Soft Money," *Washington Post*, July 18, 1996, p. A8.

7. Thomas Ferguson and Joel Rogers, *Right Turn: The Decline of the Democrats and the Future of American Politics*, New York: Hill and Wang, 1986.

8. Wayne, "Soft Money."

9. Kevin Phillips, *Arrogant Capital*, p. 126.

10. Figures on Arkansas millionaires and billionaires and business relationships from *Forbes*'s billionaire issue, October 1997.

11. David Maraniss, *First in His Class*, New York: Simon & Schuster, 1995, p. 369.

12. On Riady family empire and connection to the Stephens empire, Rose Law, etc., Holman W. Jenkins, Jr., "Business World: They Always Believed in Jarkansas," *Wall Street Journal*, October 22, 1996, p. A23.

13. Ibid.

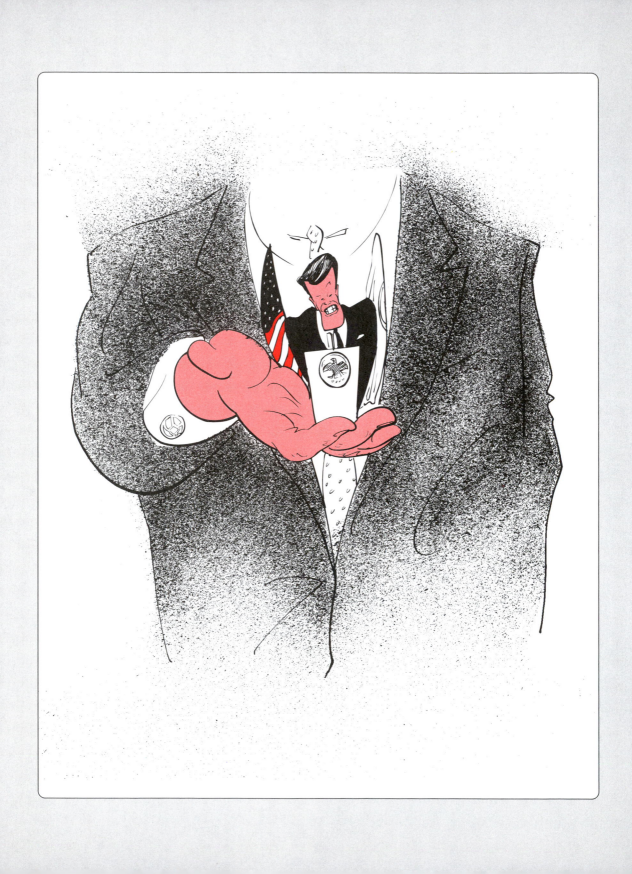

THE MAINTENANCE OF PRIVILEGE

What is surprising is that the privileged should always be so few. Since social advancement does exist, and since this tiny elite has always depended on the surplus provided by the non-privileged, when the surplus increased, the tiny minority ought to have expanded, too. But it never has, even in the 20th century.

—FERNAND BRAUDEL,
Civilization and Capitalism

Bill Clinton mastered the art of hustling the big money that is indispensable for getting elected to high office in the United States, but he did it the hard way. While it is possible for a man of modest means and great ambitions to ascend to the pinnacle of leadership in the United States, members of the American upper class use a simpler and steadier route to power.

Throughout the twentieth century, the rich have maintained a number of elite institutions and practices that prepare their children to lead the nation. A number of American presidents in this century came directly from this tiny minority: Teddy Roosevelt, William Howard Taft, Franklin Delano Roosevelt, John F. Kennedy, and George Bush. But there is a more important way in which the elite take part in national leadership. Almost all presidents—including self-made men like Dwight D. Eisenhower and Ronald Reagan, who first succeeded outside the realms of politics and business—have surrounded themselves with close associates who come directly from upper-class circles.

When George Bush ascended to the presidency in 1992, the situation seemed extreme because he brought along personal friends—James Baker, Nicholas Brady, and Robert Mosbacher—to run his cabinet. Not only did these men share Bush's upper-class background and training, but they also had a collective net worth of about $250 million. In fact, the makeup of the cabinet was not unusual. Studies have shown that the majority of cabinet members have come from elite circles:

205 INDIVIDUALS SERVED IN PRESIDENTIAL CABINETS FROM 1897–1972[1]
60%—were members of the upper-class social elite
78%—were members of the business elite (serving on corporate boards of directors or working in corporate law firms)
50%—were both of the above

Where Did the Elite Come From?

The United States has always been a country with great distinctions between rich and poor. But when the nation was founded, it was much more egalitarian than any of the Old World countries from which the settlers were emigrating. Although candidates for our highest offices in the early years of the Republic were usually rich landowners, like Washington and Jefferson, the independence of the young nation and the fate of its democratic institutions depended on the existence of a new kind of "middle class" that had little power in the authoritarian aristocracies of Europe. In 1776 this middle class was made up of the large percentage of men who were small farmers, artisans, and shop-

keepers, people who held modest amounts of property and wealth and had control over their own work. It was only with this semblance of equality among small property holders in an agricultural society that it was possible to create the traditions of New England town meetings and a democratically elected House of Representatives.

In the parts of the United States that were not dominated by the slave economy—the Middle Atlantic and New England states—small property holders exerted influence in society because the distribution of wealth was much more equal at the time of the Revolution than it is today.[2]

THE INCREASING CONCENTRATION OF WEALTH IN THE UNITED STATES			
	1774	1870	1989
Assets Owned by the Top 10%	45%	66%	72%
Assets Owned by the Other 90%	55%	34%	28%

Things had clearly changed by 1870, as agrarian democracy was replaced with industrial capitalism. In the second half of the nineteenth century a rising group of capitalists and industrialists, the greatest of them known as the Robber Barons, came to dominate American life. As they ruthlessly exploited every chance to control the various sectors of American society, they sought to legitimize themselves as the true and worthy "upper class." This trend has only worsened over time, for the top 10 percent controls even more wealth today than it did in 1870.

Maintaining an Aristocracy

As the rich exercised the new power of industrial capitalism in the 1870s and 1880s, they created many institutions and social structures to protect their wealth and promote their exclusive status. What is remark-able is that most of these social props, anti-quated as they seem, still survive in some form today and help maintain the aura of authority that allows the rich to domi-nate the rest of the population. Sociologist E. Digby Bartzell, a self-proclaimed member of the Philadelphia "aristocracy," subjected these upper-class institutions to lengthy analysis. He listed some of the important exclusive practices that arose in the 1880s and that have continued to define the upper class right up to the present day.[3]

• The rich sent their children to elite pri-vate schools where they could be protected from association with children of other classes. Old schools like Andover, Exeter, and St. Paul's became popular in the early 1880s. Over the next twenty years, they were fol-lowed by a new crop of exclusive prep schools, including Groton, Taft, Hotchkiss, and Choate.

• The upper class began to meet to play games—usually golf and tennis—at exclusive clubs. The Country Club was first estab-lished in Brookline, Massachusetts, in 1882; one or more such clubs were soon con-structed in every large metropolitan area.

• The rich escaped to exclusive summer resort communities: Northeast Harbor, and Kennebunkport, Maine; Newport, Rhode Island; and others.

• They left the cities for remote suburban residential areas: Tuxedo Park (New York), followed by Chestnut Hill (Boston), Shaker Heights (Cleveland), and many more.

• Parents wanted their children, graduates of the exclusive prep schools, to mix with young men of similar origins, so they sent them to the prestigious universities of Yale, Harvard, and Princeton. The list also included the rest of the Ivy League and a host of small, exclusive colleges.

• The Social Register, first published in 1887 in New York City, was a list of the families with whom the very wealthy felt it accept-able to associate; it also served as a source-book for debutante daughters making their social "debuts" and beginning their search for proper upper-class husbands. The Register was published in separate editions for the elite families of thirteen American cities; one large edition now covers the whole country.

• The "men's club" was born as a meeting place for men of business affairs in major American cities—for instance, the Century, Metropolitan, and Links clubs in New York; the Bohemian in San Francisco.

There were and are, of course, many other ways for the upper class to preserve its privi-lege. "High culture" is often purchased through large-scale philanthropic donations to symphonies, art museums, and histori-cal organizations (some historical sites are nothing more than lavish mansions devoted to the acquisitions of one family, such as the Vanderbilts or Hearsts). In the realm of pri-vate philanthropy, about half of all money donated comes from multimillionaires. Although some charitable programs help the needy and neglected, the fact is that American philanthropy is not primarily devoted to such causes.

Charitable philanthropy directly serves the rich. Teresa Odendahl, in her book *Charity Begins at Home*, calculated that over two thirds of philanthropic giving goes to "elite non-profit institutions—Ivy League universities, museums, symphonies, think-tanks, private hospitals, prep schools, and the like." Through such donations, which are invariably tax-deductible, "the wealthy end up funding their own interests."[4] Of the $124 billion spent on private philanthropy in 1991, only 10 percent went for "human service" projects that serve the poor. Furthermore, as the richest citizens began making more money they began giving away less of it. In 1979 individuals who earned more than $1 million gave away about 7 percent of their after-tax income; by 1996, that figure had fallen to just 4 percent.[5] Likewise, it should come as no surprise that in 1995, when corporate profits jumped a record of 30 percent to over $600 billion, corporate philanthropy went up only 8 percent, accounting for just $7 billion of the $144 billion given by all sources.[6]

The Foundation of Public Opinion

The corporate rich have another philanthropic outlet that allows them to influence the political arena. G. William Domhoff, in his various studies of the upper class and the "power elite," reached the conclusion that rich donors "spent far more on their horses and dogs than they did on politics."[7] He meant that most upper-class individuals have expensive hobbies that they find more exciting than direct involvement in electioneering. For this reason, indirect methods of concentrating the resources of the upper class have been devised; among them are the numerous elite policy-discussion groups, nonprofit foundations, and research institutes funded by the largest fortunes.

The staying power of great industrial fortunes has been formidable when they've been invested in such places as the Ford Foundation, the Rockefeller Foundation, and the Carnegie Corporation. These organizations are devoted to exploring and recommending new directions in public policy; while they generally support the agenda of the corporate world in business matters, they are often liberal on social issues regarding race and gender, a point of great consternation to many conservatives.

Among the older philanthropic organizations there are also those, such as the Lilly Foundation and the Pew Memorial Trust, that fund more conservative approaches. Just before Ronald Reagan was elected, two new foundations began delineating far-right social policies for the United States—the American Enterprise Institute and the Heritage Foundation, the latter formed by Joseph Coors and Richard Mellon Scaife, heirs to two of America's richest fortunes and supporters of the Religious Right. The Heritage Foundation differs from other charitable foundations in spending a larger portion of its budget, about 60 percent, on putting out an explicitly political message. According to the *Wall Street Journal*, the Heritage Foundation, "more than other think tanks, has extended its political influence by spending more money on raising funds and promoting its thoughts than on researching them."[8]

Related to the big foundations are the policy groups such as the Council on Foreign Relations, which publishes the journal *Foreign Affairs* and selects promising politicians and academics to rub shoulders with America's corporate and investment leaders. One half of the group's members come from the New York City area, where they represent the economic powerhouses of finance and industry.[9] This moderately conservative organization seeks to keep the worldwide capitalist system running smoothly and protect and expand open investment patterns around the globe. Its counterparts in influencing domestic economic policy, which are also dominated by the very biggest corporations, are the Business Council and the Council for Economic Development.

To many critics on the right and left, this kind of upper-class cooperation looks like an immensely powerful conspiracy. The far-right critique suggests that the Council on Foreign Relations is secretly selling out the United States to foreign interests. In reality it is a relatively transparent organization where elite leaders openly gather opinions about how to proceed on key issues of public policy. G. William Domhoff has explained how academic experts serve the group: "The experts involved in the policy issue were not working independently. They were working for a ruling-class organization that had hired them to provide corporate leaders with the best possible advice they could suggest for making corporate capitalism function more smoothly and expansively."[10] The Council on Foreign Relations has operated with a much lower profile in the 1990s. Its agenda, the opening of world markets and the globalization of commerce, is now firmly established and enforced by the operations of the World Bank and the International Monetary Fund.

Members of the upper-class corporate and banking families can be quite candid about their special right to intervene in the political process. Stewart Alsop (he and his brother Joseph were products of the upper class and two of America's most influential syndicated newspaper columnists from the 1930s to the 1970s) put it this way: "I suspect that a great power needs an elite, a class of self-confident and more or less disinterested people who are accustomed to running things."[11]

Change or No Change?
Will Elite Organizations Survive?

Skull and Bones is a small, secret society at Yale University. During the late nineteenth century and the first half of the twentieth century it was home to many rich, white Anglo-Saxon Protestant young men who went on to run the country, including William Howard Taft, Republican president from 1908 to 1912; Averell Harriman, the leading financier of the Democratic Party from 1932 to 1992; Prescott Bush, the manager of Harriman's bank, Republican senator, and father of George Bush; and George Bush, Republican president from 1988 to 1992. The list could be filled out with the names of scores of very influential Americans—for example, Henry Stimson, Republican financier and two-time secretary of war, and Henry Luce, the nation's leading publisher (*Time, Life, Fortune,* etc.).

In the first half of the twentieth century, George Bush's father and his generation of Bonesmen were intimately involved in maintaining family wealth, looking after the welfare of America's largest banks and corporations, running the affairs of both political parties, and directing U.S. foreign and domestic policies.

When George Bush made the long ascent to the nation's highest office, he was aided by some of the same Eastern Establishment ties, but they were not as dominant as they had been in the mid-twentieth century. National wealth and power can no longer be concentrated in a place so small as one college club; after a reign of nearly a hundred years, the leadership of America's old elite must make room for contending forces.

By no means is the upper-class static, since one of its purposes is to honor new wealth and keep it circulating within elite circles. In recent years the transformation of the American and global economies has yielded bonanzas to the biggest CEOs, Wall Street traders, and corporate lawyers, as well as to entrepreneurial wizards in new technologies and marketing strategies; now they can enjoy upper-class status, too. Rich white Anglo-Saxon Protestant families do not have as much control over the old upper-class institutions as they once did. Wealthy families of Jewish, Irish, and Italian heritage, among others, have found ways to purchase some degree of influence over upper-class tastes and interactions. Many of the oldest country clubs now permit them to swing golf clubs next to WASPS. Racial barriers are more difficult to overcome. In 1994 the chairman of General Motors, John Smith, took the unusual and brave step of resigning from the Bloomfield Hills Country Club outside of Detroit because it would not admit a high-ranking black auto executive. But a great many private clubs still exclude African-Americans, despite the commercially viable stardom of the young black golfer Tiger Woods. After reviewing the policies of six thousand private golf clubs in the United States, Charles Dorton of the Sports Opportunity and Information Center reported that "most of the private clubs have no black members, or just one, to qualify for the PGA Tour."[12]

The rich cannot control every aspect of American culture, nor are they immune to the sentiments generated by movements toward racial and sexual equality. While upper-class individuals still dominate the elite institutions of higher learning—sitting on boards of trustees, donating new buildings and facilities, and endowing prestigious academic chairs—they are not necessarily averse to opening up the system. Yale University is no longer just a school for rich white boys, and Skull and Bones actually voted to admit women as members in 1991 (but not without a fight from some of the old guard—ultraconservative member William F. Buckley joined a lawsuit in an attempt to block the women's entry). Although Ivy League schools still depend heavily on gifts from rich alumni,

some of these people graduated in the 1960s and 1970s, a period when the liberalization of American society put more emphasis on achievement than on bloodlines or money. Public commitment to education, through the GI Bill and a host of other government programs, made it possible for an increasing number of working- and middle-class youth to attend college, even at the most elite institutions. Gone were the years described by Theodore H. White, the presidential historian, when he and the handful of less affluent students at Harvard were called "meatballs" and regarded as "a zoo of specimens of the mobile lower middle class."

But this may prove to be a short-lived phenomenon. Recently a research group formed by thirty-one of the most selective colleges found that government scholarship aid to their students was declining fast, from 36 percent of all grants awarded in 1979 to just 18 percent in 1995. The schools, most of them well endowed, were making up much of the shortfall from their own funds, but increasingly they were giving fewer scholarships to working- and lower-middle-class students in need of substantial aid packages. Andrew Delbanco, the Levi Professor of Humanities at Columbia, discerned a trend of "scholarships for the rich," and described how some schools were buying lists of high school students with strong S.A.T. scores and then sorting out the ones with desirable ZIP codes—that is, towns and neighborhoods known to house affluent people. "There is talk," he said, "that median family income among financial-aid recipients is rising suspiciously fast."[13]

What Comes Next?

Before writing off Skull and Bones and similar organizations as anachronisms belonging to a past era, one might wait to see if "old money" isn't regenerated by the growing inequality in the land. Perhaps new millionaires and billionaires will join or replicate the established social networks of influence.

At the Democratic National Convention in 1988, there was a key moment that illustrated the staying power of the upper class. When Michael Dukakis finished his speech accepting the presidential nomination, few Americans were aware that they were witnessing a rare, open demonstration of deference to the power that lurks behind the "democratic" facade of American political life. The first person allowed to come out and share the podium, holding up Dukakis's hand in victory, was none other than Mrs. Pamela Harriman, the widow of Averell Harriman. She gained this honor because under the Harrimans' leadership rich Democrats had started to push the party rightward in the early 1980s; their small but influential organization,

"Democrats for the '80s," was instrumental in picking Dukakis as the top dog in 1988. Her group renamed itself "Democrats for the '90s" and latched onto the Democratic Leadership Council and Bill Clinton. Even though Averell Harriman died in 1986, his residual power as the establishment figure who had bankrolled the Democratic Party since the 1930s helped elect Clinton in 1992.

At the Democratic convention in 1996, Clinton was an uncontested incumbent and no one of the stature of Averell and Pamela Harriman was visibly pulling the strings in the upper ranks of the party. But at the 1996 Republican convention, the heirs to the old establishment looked quite prominent and familiar. George Walker Bush, governor of Texas and son of the former President, was comfortably running the convention proceedings with another offspring of eastern investment bankers, Christine Todd Whitman, governor of New Jersey.

1. Beth Mintz, "The President's Cabinet, 1897–1972," *Insurgent Sociologist*, Spring 1975.

2. David M. Gordon, *What's Wrong with the U.S. Economy?*, Boston: South End Press, 1982, p. 32.

3. E. Digby Bartzell, *The Protestant Establishment: Aristocracy and Class in America*, New York: Random House, 1964; and *An American Business Aristocracy*, New York: Collier, 1962.

4. Teresa Odendahl, *Charity Begins at Home: Generosity and Self-Interest among the Philanthropic Elite*, New York: Basic Books, 1990. The quotation comes from her op-ed piece "A Thousand Pointless Lights," *New York Times*, August 4, 1990.

5. Randy Albelda and Nancy Folbre, *The War on the Poor*, New York: The New Press, 1996, p. 90.

6. *New York Times*, May 24, 1996, p. A24.

7. G. William Domhoff, *The Power Elite and the State*, New York: Aldine de Gruyter, 1990.

8. Christopher Georges, "Conservative Heritage Foundation Finds Recipe for Influence: Ideas

and Marketing = Clout," *Wall Street Journal*, August 10, 1995, p. A10.

9. G. William Domhoff, *Who Rules America Now?*, Englewood Cliffs, NJ: Prentice Hall, 1983, p. 87. Included in the Council on Foreign Relations:
23 of the 25 top corporations
21 of the 25 top banks
16 of the 25 top insurance companies
16 directors from Morgan Guaranty Trust
15 directors from Chase Manhattan Bank
10 directors from Citibank
14 of 17 trustees of the Rockefeller Foundation
10 of 17 trustees of the Carnegie Corporation
7 of 16 trustees of the Ford Foundation

10. *The Power Elite and the State*, p. 183.

11. Stewart Alsop, *Stay of Execution*, New York: Lippincott, 1979.

12. Lawrence Otis Graham, "The One and Only Tiger Woods," *New York Times*, Editorial Page, August 31, 1996.

13. Andrew Delbanco, "Scholarships for the Rich," *New York Times Magazine*, September 1, 1996, p. 37.

AUTHORITARIAN

DEMOCRACY

It is the unvarying law that the wealth of the community will be in the hands of the few.

—DAVID J. BREWER, *Supreme Court Justice,* 1893[1]

When Cold War tensions with the Soviet Union disappeared at the end of the 1980s, the frightening vision of "the evil empire" no longer served to distract our citizens from the distressing realities of economic inequality. As a short-term diversion, Saddam Hussein was built up into a Hitler substitute by the media, but most Americans were never convinced that his weak regime posed any real danger.

While it is possible that we will again resurrect the Japanese, the Chinese, or worse yet, Asians in general as the "Yellow Peril,"

American anger is likely to be focused in a different, more ominous direction. Our patriotic fervor is now being turned inward, in search of evil aliens at home. New authoritarianism, sanctimonious attention to the flag, and ever-more obvious appeals to racism were found in the increasingly strident conservatism that evolved during the 1980s. By the first half of the 1990s, there was extraordinary enthusiasm for right-wing talk shows featuring virulent personalities such as Rush Limbaugh and G. Gordon Liddy. Popular expressions of anger and hatred were apparent throughout American culture, sometimes accompanied by eruptions of violence.

• The Religious Right spewed a steady stream of epithets at advocates of abortion. Attacks against clinics and their personnel rose from 52 in 1988 to 267 in 1993.

• A militia movement using extreme antigovernment rhetoric drew primarily on the marginalized, working-class white population. Members and supporters stockpiled military weaponry, sent letter bombs to liberal judges and lawyers, engaged in bank robberies, and sought to intimidate public officials throughout the nation. One set of sympathizers, operating on the fringe of the movement, staged the massive bombing of the Federal Building in Oklahoma City.

• Random hate crimes were perpetrated against people perceived to be "different," particularly Latino and Asian immigrants, African-Americans, and gays and lesbians. There were arson attacks on thirty-one African-American churches in the South between 1989 and 1996, fifteen of them occurring between December 1995 and May 1996.

• In many places the majority of people advocated legal means of punishing or discriminating against expressions of sexuality. Teenagers were sent to jail for fornication in Idaho. Citizens of the state of Colorado passed a referendum justifying discrimination against gays and lesbians.

By the mid-1990s, the American social and political landscape had changed so much that forces formerly on the margins of conservatism were now mainstream. The Christian Coalition, which had fewer than 5,000 members in 1989, grew to 1.7 million members in a couple of thousand chapters by 1996, and became the respectable grassroots organizing mechanism for the Republican Party.[2] When populist economic issues were raised during the 1996 election campaign, it was the right wing, not the left, that did the most effective job of exploiting them. Pat Buchanan, who had written celebrations of free trade and driven a Mercedes during the 1980s, was now attacking big business: "General Motors has become a transnational corporation that sees its future in low-wage countries and in abandoning American factories."[3]

When Buchanan playfully contemplated an attack of "pitchfork-wielding commoners" against "the castles" of the investing class, he was eased out of the campaign picture by Christian Coalition director Ralph Reed and establishment Republicans. This conflict between populism and authoritarianism within the Republican Party was not a sign of weakness; rather it demonstrated that ultraconservatives had taken over a great deal of social and political territory and that the various forces of the right had plenty of room to jockey for leadership.

Fascism Lite?

Astute social commentators had been anticipating this rightward shift since the early 1980s. Bertram Gross predicted, in his book *Friendly Fascism*, that the United States might arrive at a gentler form of the virulent ultranationalism, antilabor activity, and racism which coalesced into fascism in Europe in the 1930s.[4] Corporate America would tolerate such a rightward drift, so the argument went, because more government restrictions on personal freedom would enhance business efforts to discipline the labor force and increase corporate profits.

This critique had its counterpart in a well-articulated viewpoint coming from the center-right. Kevin Phillips's book *Post-Conservative America* suggested that populist concern in grassroots America might be focused either on economic equality or on a reactionary social agenda.[5] He pointed out the similarities between the ideas of the New Right in America and the beliefs of the European "Conservative Revolutionaries" of the early 1900s, which made possible the rise of fascism. Both were: 1) extremely nationalistic and patriotic, and partial to authoritarian solutions; 2) antisecular, and antihumanist, taking their inspiration from newly invented "traditional" religion; 3) antiliberal and supportive of a restoration of "old morality." When analyzing the growing strength of the Republican Party, especially in the South, Phillips cautioned that "any Sun Belt hegemony over our politics has a unique potential . . . to accommodate a drift toward apple-pie authoritarianism."

Ironically, Phillips, as an adviser to Richard Nixon in 1968, had helped map out the "Southern Strategy" that was partly responsible for this shift. Republicans had been impressed by the strengths of third-party candidate George Wallace in 1968 and decided to cater to the social conservatism of many white voters, both southerners and northerners, who otherwise were quite satisfied with the Democrats and their New Deal politics. The successful Republican strategy, which later stooped to open race-baiting, lured many southern white Protestants and northern ethnic voters away from their 150-year allegiance to the Democratic Party. By 1996, the Republican Party was led by southerners: Speaker of the House Newt Gingrich of Georgia; Senate Majority Leader Trent Lott of Mississippi; House Majority Leader Dick Armey of Texas. Apparently the Sun Belt's move to the forefront of American politics—political analyst Samuel Lobell called this "the mechanization of the Southern Baptists"—was complete.

It is possible that the next economic downturn—or stock market crash—will bring on further developments. During the recession at the end of the 1980s, ex–Ku Klux Klan leader David Duke gathered strong support from disgruntled citizens in Louisiana for his gubernatorial and U.S. Senate races. Voters did not seem to be bothered by his record, which included plenty of statements like: "The Jews have been working against our national interest. . . . I think they should be punished."[6]

Bertram Gross and Kevin Phillips had each foreseen part of a process that engendered remarkable tolerance for authoritarian political solutions. Gross correctly identified the kind of authority that the corporate world wanted to exercise over working- and middle-class Americans. Phillips was perceptive about the way ordinary Americans would participate in actually constructing a more harsh and restrictive social milieu. By the 1990s the two strands were coalescing into somthing we could call "Authoritarian Democracy." Today it is clear that the goals of the corporate rich can be furthered by the enthusiasms of the popular classes, especially in the realms of religion.

The New Christian Fundamentalism

Many Americans are attracted to the kind of Christian fundamentalism that advocates the reestablishment of a "Christian nation" in the United States. Their concern about the moral order of society and family values is understandable, for families are under a great deal of stress, and both children and adults are overexposed to corporate commercialism. Because the larger culture seems devoid of trust and commitment, and is fragmented by rapid social change, many people turn to new religious institutions to fill the void.

The most influential of these is the new current of Christian Fundamentalism that has emerged from the broad evangelical Protestant culture that includes 25 percent of all Americans. From various evangelical influences—including Southern Baptists, charismatics, Pentecostals, holiness churches, and other fundamentalist traditions—millions of people have fashioned a new fundamentalism that stresses belief in biblical inerrancy, pastoral authority, male superiority, and the idea that the United States must be governed according to their religious principles.[7] Many also express themselves politically through the large network of conservative political organizations known as the Religious Right (which also harbors a sizable number of very conservative Catholics).

Protestantism has always been adaptable to the changing needs of American society. In nineteenth-century Evangelicalism, there was an emphasis on submission to authority and good Christian work habits that delighted the owners of capital, who often established "mission" churches in their factory towns so that evangelical preachers could instruct the men, women, and children who labored for them.[8] Today, the emphasis on authority still remains, but fresh elements have been added into the fundamentalist mix that reflect the kind of capitalist consumer culture that exists at the end of the twentieth century.

In particular, from the middle-class charismatic Christians comes a belief in the powers of the Holy Spirit to meet the material needs of individuals and endow them with "blessings" of wealth and good health.

The new faith bears an uncanny resemblance to the mysterious ways that billionaires prosper in our present era of finance capitalism. George Gilder, one of the intellectual authors of supply-side economics, once described his ideal economy in preacherly tones: "Capitalist production engenders faith—in one's neighbors, in one's society, and in the compensatory logic of the cosmos. Search and you shall find, give and you will be given unto, supply creates its own demand."[9]

Other business gurus, who may have no affiliation with the religious movement, are happy to make use of the religious metaphors. In 1996 Sanford I. Weill, the CEO of the giant financial conglomerate known as The Traveler's Group, staged a "revival-like convention" for his Primerica Financial Services subsidiary, according to *Fortune* magazine. Forty thousand salespeople came from around the country at their own expense to hear Weill tell them that there is no limit to the riches they can amass. The giant banners that flanked the stage read: "Great Crusade to the Summit."

Such affinities help explain why the Christian Coalition can throw itself wholeheartedly into supporting conservative Republican goals even though it doesn't necessarily have the same priorities as the rich. The Religious Right probably embraces antiabortion politics more passionately than any other issue, yet many rich Americans do not (in fact, the favorite philanthropic cause of many wealthy conservatives is population control). One impact of the abortion issue is that the rights of the unborn seem to have grown at the expense of concern for the health and welfare of millions of already born children; the enthusiasm of the antiabortionists has often been manipulated by those who want to eliminate government programs that spend tax money on any kind of human welfare.

The opposition to abortion is also linked to the desire of the fundamentalists to control the lives of women in other ways. A clear call to reassert male dominance was issued by a lay group called the "Promise Keepers," which started drawing overflow crowds to America's football stadiums in 1995 and 1996. An offshoot of James Dobson's Focus on the Family and other right-wing Christian groups, the all-male Promise Keepers are vociferously pro-God, pro-family, pro-America, and antihomosexual and claim to be "reclaiming our manhood." They reassert their biblical right to patriarchal control over their households, following the credo: "Treat the lady gently and lovingly. But lead!"[10]

These restrictive manifestations of the religious revival—the pro-male spectacles staged by the Promise Keepers, the calls for governmental prohibitions on abortion, increased demands for book-banning in school libraries, the insistence on teaching abstinence-only sexual education in place of birth control—are ways that people are being conditioned to accept the imposition of authority. Thus large segments of the population are inviting more intervention in their lives, not only by the churches, but also by the state and corporations.

Corporate Power Upheld by the Courts

The Supreme Court has also helped to impose social control. Although it was a champion of civil and individual rights in the tenure of the Warren Court, the Court has more often played an important role in suppressing the rights and welfare of working Americans by championing the prerogatives of the wealthy. After the Civil War, as the United States economy came under the control of corporations and the newly emergent upper class of stockholders, the Supreme Court acted to protect the freedom of corporations to invest and make money without hindrance.

During the era of the Robber Barons, the Court made use of the 14th Amendment, which, ironically, had originally been written to guarantee citizenship and equal civil rights to ex-slaves at the end of the Civil War. The Court invoked the amendment to define the corporation as a "person" under the law. This meant that government could not interfere with the activities of this corporate "person" lest it be guilty of abridging citizens' rights. This interpretation came in response to the fact that in the 1880s many states and localities were trying to limit corporate power, protect the rights and health of workers, and encourage public alternatives to corporate ownership. The Court granted corporations their almost unlimited power with the *Santa Clara* decision of 1886, in which it sided with the Union Pacific Railroad in its struggle to escape regulation by the state of California. In the same year the Court invalidated 230 other state laws that had been passed to regulate corporations. Justice David J. Brewer clarified the defining issue during a speech to the New York Bar Association in 1893, when he said: "It is the unvarying law that the wealth of the community will be in the hands of the few."[11]

From the time of the Civil War to the tenure of Franklin Roosevelt, the majority of justices, men from upper-class backgrounds and/or corporate law practices, were sympathetic toward this interpretation of the Constitution. At the same time the Court was reluctant to use the 14th Amendment for its original intent, which was to protect African-Americans, and it was not until the 1954 *Brown v. Board of Education* decision that the Supreme Court began to strike down most of the state and local laws that allowed segregation and discrimination. According to Justice Hugo Black, writing in 1939:

> Of the cases in this Court in which the Fourteenth Amendment was applied during the first fifty years after its adoption, less than one-half of one percent invoked it in protection of the Negro race, and more than fifty percent asked that its benefits be extended to corporations.[12]

States' Rights or Workers' Rights?

Now that corporate power is long established in all states, states' rights are again being promoted by the Supreme Court. Chief Justice William Rehnquist calls it "the new Federalism," whose purpose is to defend corporations against restrictions that might be imposed by Congress. In 1975 Rehnquist wrote about "a concept of constitutional federalism which should . . . limit federal power under the Commerce Clause" (the constitutional provision that gives Congress the power to regulate interstate commerce). The following year, as an associate justice, he led an attack (*National League of Cities v. Usery*) that simultaneously limited congressional control and restricted the rights of workers; states were told that they did not have to comply with the minimum-wage/maximum-hours provisions of the Fair Labor Standards Act.

Because the largest corporations command resources that are usually sufficient to overwhelm government at the state level, the rhetoric of states' rights really justifies corporate license. Theodore Roosevelt had noted this problem nearly a century earlier when he sought to bust the trusts: "The effective fight against adequate Government control and supervision of individual, and especially of corporate, wealth engaged in interstate business is chiefly done under cover of an appeal to states' rights."[13]

Today, thanks to the appointments of Ronald Reagan, George Bush, and Bill Clinton, the Supreme Court is again a conservative body whose majority is most sympathetic to the rights and privileges of corporations. A number of recent or upcoming judicial decisions should be considered in this light:

- Courts have allowed a vast increase in lie-detector and drug testing by business and government, a clear invasion of privacy. Everyone from athletes to State Department officials have been subjected to random drug tests.

- The Supreme Court has reversed affirmative action decisions and denied the premise of "equal pay for equal work" in sex discrimination cases.

- Federal and state legislatures are being lobbied heavily by the giant corporations to pass laws which will restrict the use of class-action suits to punish negligent companies that injure their workers or the general public.

- Corporate appointees to the National Labor Relations Board virtually eliminated the legal remedies of labor unions during the Reagan and Bush administrations and made it difficult to protest illegal behavior by employers. Although the Clinton administration has made the NLRB slightly less obstructionist, the Supreme Court has seldom been inclined to review the anti-labor behavior of corporations. Strikes have become rarer than ever because corporations are now free to fire employees who go on strike and bring in permanent replacements. Such practices, as long as they are tolerated by the courts, will virtually outlaw the right to strike.

• In the *Buckley v. Valeo* decision of 1976, the Court allowed wealthy individuals to spend an unlimited amount on political campaigns, ruling that it was a matter of free speech; this ruling may soon be expanded to allow unrestricted corporate gifts.[14]

The conservative orientation of the Supreme Court has been supported by an even more conservative shift in the study of law. In 1972, Lewis Powell, shortly before he was elevated to the Supreme Court, sent a note to the U.S. Chamber of Commerce urging the business community to "buy the top academic reputations of the country to add credibility to corporate studies and give business a stronger voice on the campus."[15] Businesses and conservative foundations did just that, by backing university programs that emphasized "Law and Economics," a curriculum that is related to the Public Choice (or Rational Choice) theory. Law and Economics teaches that all human activity is based on the pursuit of individual self-interest in the marketplace and that the law itself ought to closely adhere to market and corporate values.

This reduction of all human activities and values to computations of time and money exercises a profound influence today on the nation's legal schools. The Olin Foundation funded Law and Economics programs at Yale University to the tune of $1.5 million; at Harvard, Stanford, and the University of Chicago for $1 million each; Duke, MIT, and the Universities of Pennsylvania and Virginia were in the half-million-dollar category. The foundation proclaimed that its gifts were "intended to strengthen the economic, political, and cultural institutions upon which . . . private enterprise is based."[16]

Economic and political analyst Robert Kuttner explained that private foundations were willing to pay so handsomely for Public Choice and Law and Economics programs because they "are reinforcing of the laissez-faire ideal and thus very congenial to society's most powerful."[17]

The Olin Foundation not only paid to institute this kind of education at such law schools as Harvard and Yale, but it also supported a variety of scholars who argued for a narrowed conception of democracy and freedom in other fields. One recipient of Olin largesse was Harvard professor Samuel Huntington, who was awarded $1.4 million. He had written on the governability of democracies for the Trilateral Commission in 1975 and had anticipated the agenda of corporate America in the last quarter of the twentieth century:

Some of the problems of governance in the United States stem from an excess of democracy. . . . Needed, instead, is a greater degree of moderation in democracy.

1. Howard Zinn, *A People's History of the United States*, New York: Harper & Row, 1980, p. 255.

2. Ralph Reed, *Active Faith*, New York: The Free Press, 1996.

3. *New York Times*, December 31, 1995, p. A20.

4. Bertram Gross, *Friendly Fascism*, New York: M. Evans and Company, 1980.

5. Kevin Phillips, *Post-Conservative America*, New York: Random House, 1982.

6. Southern Poverty Law Center, "Klanwatch" newsletter, Spring 1990.

7. For more on the evolution of fundamentalist Christian beliefs, see Chapters Two and Three of Steve Brouwer, Susan D. Rose, and Paul Gifford, *Exporting the American Gospel: Global Christian*

Fundamentalism, New York and London: Routledge, 1996.

8. For classic depictions of early industry and cultural influences of religion, see Edward P. Thompson, *The Making of the English Working Class*, Hammondsworth: Penguin, 1968, and Anthony Wallace, *Rockdale*, New York: W.W. Norton, 1978.

9. Quoted in Phillips, *Post-Conservative America*.

10. Tony Evans, *Seven Promises of a Promise Keeper*, quoted by Joe Conason, Alfred Ross, and Lee Cokorinos, "The Promise Keepers Are Coming: The Third Wave of the Religious Right," *The Nation*, October 7, 1996, pp. 11–19.

For insights into the new Christian fundamentalism as a globalizing religion, see Steve Brouwer, Susan D. Rose, and Paul Gifford, *Exporting the American Gospel: Global Christian Fundamentalism*, New York and London: Routledge, 1996.

11. Zinn, p. 255.

12. David Dale Martin, "The Corporation and Anti-Trust Law Policy," in Warren J. Samuels and Arthur S. Miller, eds., *Corporations and Society: Power and Responsibility*, Westport, CT: Greenwood Press, 1987, p. 212.

13. Herman Schwartz, "Same Old States' Rights Song," *The Nation*, October 14, 1996, p. 14.

14. Recently retired senator Bill Bradley has been fighting a lonely battle against such rulings, writing that "money is not speech," and in fact that it can eliminate freedom of expression because "the powerful continue to broadcast their voices, while the less powerful cannot be heard." *New York Times*, November 1996, Opinion Page.

15. Quoted in Noam Chomsky and Edward S. Herman, *Manufacturing Consent*, New York: Pantheon, 1988.

16. Jon Wiener, "Dollars for Neocon Scholars," *The Nation*, January 1, 1990.

17. Robert Kuttner, *Everything for Sale*, New York: Knopf, 1996, p. 341.

PART

IV

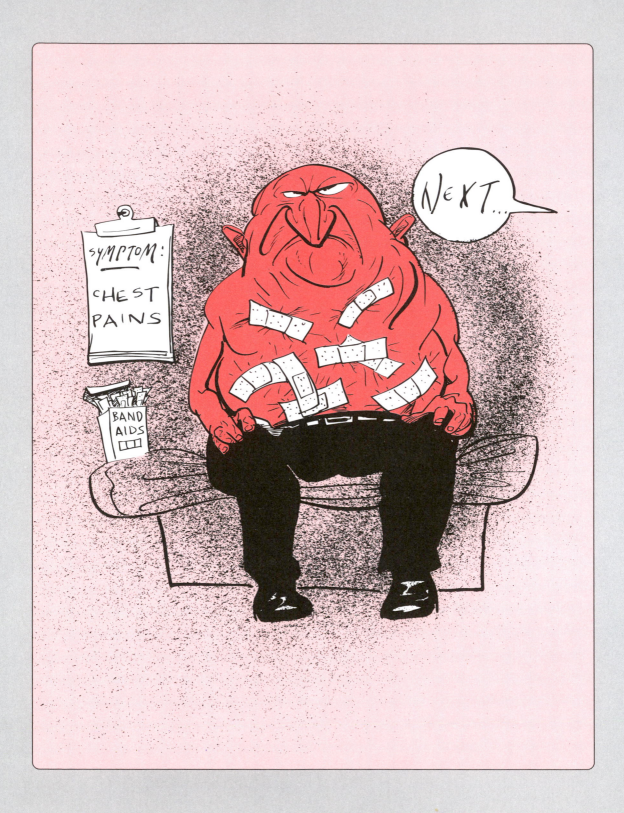

WORKING IN A
FAIR SOCIETY

The first three parts of this book catalogued the growing economic and social unfairness that characterized the 1980s and 1990s, and presented a brief look at how the powerful and wealthy maintain their political and social advantages. It should be clear that the United States, the world's richest nation, was not forced by circumstance to promote economic growth through increased exploitation of working people, and that furthermore, the practice of driving down wages and taking away social benefits did nothing to increase the productivity of our society.

Many of our business leaders and journalists express admiration for the rapid economic growth of authoritarian regimes in newly industrialized countries that rely on extreme levels of political repression. Instead they should be looking at other advanced industrial democracies which practiced more humane ways of overcoming the problems of stagnation. These nations continue to deliver basic services and health care to their citizens without going bankrupt; they do not doom their citizens to homelessness, nor do they create low-wage zones within their own countries; on the contrary, they have succeeded in increasing the average standard of living and the level of industrial productivity.

What's their secret?

While both political parties in the U.S. serve the interests of large corporations, in most other industrialized countries there are political parties of the left—labor, social democratic, and socialist—which represent the interests of a broad spectrum of middle-class and working-class people. In several countries these parties have enjoyed success in implementing their progressive political programs. Even where left-leaning parties long ago abandoned the project of over-throwing capitalism and have drifted rightward, they still offer a vision of a just society and insist on providing a whole set of benefits that are available to all citizens. Some conservative parties elsewhere are actually to the left of the Democratic Party in the United States. For instance, the ruling party in Germany, the Christian Democrats, is much more liberal in regard to social policy and treatment of the poor, and in 1996 took the side of workers versus employers in a battle over sick-leave benefits.

The reasons for this crucial difference between the U.S. and other industrialized countries are complex. European democracies did not begin as ours did in a newly settled country where farmers and religious dissidents proclaimed their freedom. Democratic and socialist movements emerged together in Europe with the same motive: to emancipate working people and other ordinary citizens from the centuries-old domination of society by aristocratic families who controlled both wealth and government. When truly representative democratic elections were finally permitted in Europe in the late nineteenth or early twentieth centuries, socialist and social democratic parties often won power or became strong partners in ruling coalitions.

When "social democracy" is mentioned, Americans often think of Sweden, a country that is much more egalitarian than the United States and that taxes the rich heavily in order to insure that everyone shares in economic prosperity. We Americans have a slightly higher average standard of living, but Swedish working people (the huge majority of the population) receive higher pay and are much better protected by social programs than their counterparts in the United States.

"But so what?" many Americans might wonder. "Isn't Sweden the exception, a small, utopian country that no one can hope to emulate?"

On the contrary, it is the United States which is out of the mainstream. All other major industrial countries have promoted government programs shaped by social democratic values, and have achieved egalitarian results. For instance, one very good measure of "economic democracy" that can be applied cross-culturally is to compare family incomes of those who rank in the 90th percentile (only 10 percent of the population earns more than them, making this the bottom edge of our affluent upper-middle class) with those who are in the 10th percentile (where only 10 percent of the population earns less, putting these low-paid working people on the verge of being poor). In the early 1990s, this ratio of high to low incomes in Sweden, Belgium, and the Netherlands was just under 3 to 1, meaning the "highs" made three times as much money as the "lows"; in other Western European countries and in Japan, Canada, and Australia, the ratios were between 3 to 1 and 4 to 1. Only the United States had inequality that was almost off the charts: the 90th percentile outearned the 10th by a margin of 6 to 1.[1]

There is a simple conclusion that can be drawn from this situation: other rich countries have fewer poor people. Furthermore, their poor people are not nearly as poor as those in the United States. No country has ever eliminated poverty completely, but the other industrialized countries make it much easier for people to escape from poverty quickly and to lead a dignified life in the working class.

A skeptic will surely ask: "Don't social programs that lift the poor out of poverty detract from the performance of the economy?" Apparently not. The U.S. is still richer on a per capita basis when measured against twelve other OECD (Organization for Economic Cooperation and Development) countries, but the gap has been closing rather steadily over twenty years:

PER CAPITA INCOME* OF 12 OECD COUNTRIES COMPARED WITH THE U.S.[2]			
1973	1979	1989	1994
66%	70%	75%	77%

*As measured by purchasing power of earnings

In the following chapters we will look at more international comparisons and suggest ways that we Americans can restructure our economy to bring ourselves in line with other prosperous democracies. But first let us focus on just one area, the provision of health care, where the United States is seemingly unable to provide for the general welfare of its people.

Where the Free Market Has No Business: Health Care

Change in the health industry . . . would have some of the classical aspects of the industrial revolution . . . and profitability as the mandatory condition of survival.[3]
—Dr. PAUL ELLWOOD, the health analyst who coined the term Health Maintenance Organization (HMO), 1971

The United States has the dubious distinction of spending a world-record amount, 14 percent of its gross domestic product and almost twice as much per person as anyplace else, on a health care system that does not work.

In every other advanced industrial society,

the government has provided for a national health care system through public financing or nonprofit insurance associations. These other health care systems, which are not profit-making industries, deliver better overall results: 100 percent of the people are covered; the average citizen lives longer; the infant mortality rates are lower.

At the beginning of the 1990s, the sorry state of America's medical delivery system was on everyone's mind. Polls indicated that most people were worried about the adequacy of their health insurance because they feared that major medical problems could bankrupt their families. They were also troubled by the growing number of Americans who were uninsured: 37 million in 1991.[4] Another 50 million had woefully inadequate insurance. Still others were afraid of losing their coverage if they lost their jobs; or, they were compelled to pay a greater share of the health insurance by their employers.

So, when Bill Clinton arrived in office, there was a great deal of public support for creating a simple, straightforward national health system that paid for universal care through the collection of taxes. In such a system people would continue to choose their own doctors and hospitals, but the government would set fees and arrange payments. A Harris Poll conducted in 1989 described this kind of medical care, which actually existed next door in Canada, and asked Americans if they would prefer it to the treatment they received in the United States. The results were startling: Americans preferred the Canadian system, by a margin of 61% to 27%. (Canadians also preferred their system, by a margin of 95% to 3%.[5])

There was an added attraction in the Canadian national health care program that should have clinched the deal: even though it delivered care to everyone, rich and poor alike, the Canadian system cost at least 30 percent less per capita than the U.S. system.

Even doctors believed the system had to be fixed. Although many physicians feared that their incomes might decline, 64 percent of them surveyed in a 1986 poll thought that "it is the responsibility of society, through its government, to provide everyone with the best available care." (Significantly, 74 percent suspected that their colleagues would be opposed to a national health system.[6])

There was even substantial business support for a national program, especially on the part of manufacturing giants that paid high wages and provided extensive benefits for their workers. The Chrysler Corporation endorsed the idea of national health insurance in the early 1990s, citing the staggering cost difference in providing workers with coverage in different countries. The company's own economists calculated the dollar amount that health care costs added to the price of an automobile.

HEALTH CARE COSTS PER CAR WHEN MANUFACTURED IN VARIOUS NATIONS IN 1991[7]				
U.S.	FRANCE	GERMANY	JAPAN	CANADA
$700	$375	$337	$246	$233

If It Ain't Quite Workin', Break It

In 1993 Bill and Hillary Clinton launched a highly publicized White House campaign to fix the U.S. health care system. The Clinton administration thought that a private system could be refashioned to serve all Americans, with only modest direction from the government. Their goal seemed to be to guarantee quality health care to all Americans and stop the rapid escalation of costs. But during the season of "reform" in 1993–94 the attempt

to realign the health system died, for a number of reasons.

"Managed competition" was the concept adopted by the Clinton administration on the advice of the Jackson Hole Group, an informal policy forum composed of insurance executives, business leaders, and conservative academics and supported by large grants from insurance companies.[8] Clinton was following the center-right course already charted by the Democratic Leadership Council: to provide plenty of room for big business to take part in the reorganization of the health care industry. The administration conceived government as participating in the creation of vast regional planning bodies, called Health Alliances, that were supposed to regulate competition among insurance providers and HMOs, which in turn would bid on the cost of supplying health care to groups of consumers. Through their ability to bargain for contracts with various hospitals, laboratories, suppliers, and medical groups, the HMOs, which could be either for-profit or nonprofit companies, would deliver medical services at reduced costs. Clinton's proposed bill for "managed competition" looked cumbersome and confusing to the public. No wonder, since it was 1,364 pages long.

Meanwhile the opposition political message, financed generously by the insurance industry, made its case with devastating effectiveness. Widely dispersed television ads featured scenes of "Harry and Louise," fictional middle-class characters who worried that new legislation would reduce their range of choices and diminish their coverage. By suggesting that those with good coverage (Harry and Louise) would be forced to "share" fixed amount of benefits with the poor (thus "rationing" care), the antireform lobby managed to distract the public from any reasoned analysis of the health care crisis.[9]

The Business Roundtable and the U.S. Chamber of Commerce joined the insurance industry to inundate legislators with lobbyists protesting the Clinton bill. Suddenly the legislation was dead, not even voted on in Congress.

The New Market Is Wild

The biggest reason for the failure of health care reform was that "managed care"—without government oversight—was already on the way. Managed care was an approach to medicine that relied on HMOs. In effect, a large and formerly nonprofit sector of the economy was being industrialized and commodified and turned over to capitalist interests at a very fast pace. As one might expect, the patterns of behavior were similar to those seen during earlier forms of industrialization in manufacturing, mining, and agriculture. Huge sums of money were flowing, new businesses were racing into the market, and everyone was promising a cheaper and better product.

Most new HMOs are for-profit systems, usually owned by insurance companies, which collect money from the insured and contract for the delivery of patient services with health care providers, meaning all those doctors, hospitals, laboratories, etc. that offer a health service. There is an interesting concept behind HMOs: they make a higher profit when patients are delivered less service. Because they position themselves in the middle of the cash flow, they take a large amount—the average is 14 percent—for their administrative costs. This is extremely high when compared with the overhead for government-run health programs such as Medicaid (4 percent) and Medicare (2 per-

cent), and the mere 1 percent overhead cost for the Canadian national health system. Furthermore, the HMOs and their investors want a tidy profit. Overall, 18 to 25 percent of all revenue going through the HMOs is siphoned off for administration, advertising, and profit.[10]

While the new health corporations are raking in all the money, they are not only eliminating the possibility of delivering universal health care (since there is no profit in delivering to those who can't pay), but they are degrading the level of medical practice in general. By the mid-1990s there were increasing complaints from patients and doctors all over the country that HMOs had systemized procedures for denying appropriate treatment in order to save money. As of 1996 twenty-seven states had passed laws to curb this behavior. Many HMOs actually had a "gag rule" forbidding doctors to even discuss expensive treatments with their patients, and sixteen states enacted laws prohibiting this practice. (Many HMOs still give doctors cash bonuses for reducing the number of expensive treatments prescribed. Yet if a patient should die because of lack of treatment, the HMOs cannot be sued for malpractice. Legislation to hold them accountable has been proposed.)

HMOs enjoy big savings—and rake in big profits—because of their size. When Aetna Life Insurance bought U.S. Healthcare, a giant HMO, for $8.8 billion, it formed a company that covers 23 million people, or 1 out of 12 Americans.[11] U.S. Healthcare is a strong proponent of "capitation," a formula that pays each doctor a set fee "per head"; that is, a stipulated amount covers a patient for the whole year, whether the doctor sees him or not. Critics say this encourages doctors to give as little attention to each patient as they possibly can. One physician was asked by

Aetna in 1996 to treat patients for as little as $5.25 per month and refused. He said that "these plans put you in the funny position of doing better financially if you withhold care, and that seems unethical."[12] Nearly half the primary care doctors in New York, New Jersey, and Pennsylvania are paid through such plans.

Not so long ago, in 1991–92, there were nursing shortages in many metropolitan areas and high salaries were being offered to new graduates. Students who pursued degrees in this increasingly complex profession seemed destined to find long-term employment at good wages. But by 1996, this had changed. Private for-profit hospitals and managed-care programs were putting pressure on registered nurses to speed up their work pace, then trying to replace them with nursing assistants at much lower wages.

Often, by increasing the patient-to-nurse ratio, these health facilities are able to reduce the number of registered nurses on hospital floors by as much as 25 percent. Only some of these nurses are replaced by lower-paid employees. Investor-owned hospitals employ 17 percent fewer staff members per 100 patients than not-for-profit hospitals.[13] This means less care for patients, who are generally sicker than they used to be, because managed care is treating the healthier people as outpatients or sending them home earlier. According to the former dean of the University of Pennsylvania School of Nursing, Claire M. Fagin, patients and nurses are both the losers, but not the corporations: "The cutbacks," she said, "are improving the bottom line of managed-care organizations."[14]

The *Journal of the American Medical Association* issued a disturbing report in 1996, saying that "patients who were elderly and poor were more than twice as likely to decline in health in an HMO" as in a fee-for-service plan. This report was meant to caution members of Congress as they considered turning Medicare and Medicaid patients over to HMOs in order to reduce costs.

Unleashing a Monster: The King of Private Hospitals

The Columbia/Healthcare Corporation of America bought its first hospital in 1988. After the Clinton health care reform left the field wide open for profit-making corporations, Columbia/HCA took off: its stock, valued at only $2 billion in 1992, had climbed to over $25 billion five years later. By 1996 it owned 348 hospitals, or 6.7 percent of all hospitals in the nation, and seemed well on its way toward its goal of controlling 10 percent of the nation's hospitals by the year 2000. Columbia employed 285,000 people, making it the ninth-largest private employer in the United States. In Florida it owned more than 25 percent of all hospital beds. The company was succeeding at meeting its remarkably high profit goal, a 20 percent return on annual revenues. Columbia also set up 550 home health care businesses and bought 1,400 medical practices nationwide and made them subsidiaries to its hospital system. Like other for-profit health care providers, it made the downsizing of nursing staffs a priority in order to save money.[15]

By August 1997, Columbia/HCA was in big trouble. Various charges of fraudulent behavior had been brought against fourteen senior executives, and the CEO, Richard L. Scott, was forced to resign. Federal investigators had found a systematic policy of overcharging Medicare for various services and discovered that it was linked to the incentive programs offered to the administrators of every hospital. The administrators were requiring more expensive procedures than were necessary, billing for more expensive procedures than were actually performed, or charging for medical services that were never even provided.

Evidence that something was amiss had been gathered by health industry analysts even before the indictments were served. Columbia/HCA managed to charge its patients 8 percent more than the average of all its competitors for the exact same services. It had a reputation of being a brutal competitor—a "hospital chain with brass knuckles," according to the *New York Times*. The company combined all the negative aspects of corporate behavior that have been described in earlier chapters of this book: downsizing, dishonest marketing, fraud, and systematic wage cutting.

By 1996–97, the changes in the U.S. health care system had yielded one success. The rate of increase in medical costs had slowed to just 3% annually, about the rate of inflation, and managed care could take a lot of the credit. But at what cost to the rest of society! If we were talking about some other successful product, such as telephones or fast food, there would be the expectation that people were getting a better product or that a less expensive product was being disbursed to more people. But in health care, the cost to the consumer has not yet fallen, even though fewer people are being supplied with the product and those who require expensive solutions are increasingly being denied care.

What Are the Other Options?

The cost of American health care far exceeds the amount spent by other highly developed nations:

PERCENTAGE OF GROSS DOMESTIC PRODUCT SPENT ON HEALTH CARE IN 1996[16]			
UNITED STATES	CANADA	GERMANY AND FRANCE	JAPAN AND ENGLAND
14%	10%	8% to 9%	6% to 7%

Since these other countries guarantee medical care to all while over one third of Americans—42 million people had no insurance in 1997 and 52 million had inadequate coverage—are discouraged from seeking adequate medical attention, the foregoing figures are even more dramatic.

We need to look elsewhere for answers, not just to Canada but to the rest of the industrialized world. Other nations have aging populations just as we do; in fact, Japan and all of Europe have an even higher percentage of elderly people, and they live longer than ours do. The answers to affordable health care are not to be found in private competition, which at best can hold down costs only by restricting care to fewer people.

Clear, consistent government funding and regulation are the answer. And they don't cost much. All types of administration—insurance, government oversight and bill processing, hospital management, running doctors' offices—amount to 11 percent of costs in Canada, versus 24 percent in the United States. Drugs are 50 percent cheaper in Canada. Average annual earnings for doctors are approximately $170,000 in the U.S., versus $127,000 in Canada and $80,000 in Germany.[17]

Patients in other countries enjoy much lower costs for almost every procedure and checkup, and they are entitled to more frequent care. There is no rationing.

Annual Number of Visits to the Doctor per Capita[18]

U.S.	BRITAIN	CANADA	FRANCE	ITALY	GERMANY
5.3	5.3	6.6	7.1	11	11.5

Average Number of Days per Hospital Stay

U.S.	BRITAIN	CANADA	FRANCE	ITALY	GERMANY
9.1	14.5	12.3	13.9	11.7	16.5

With such obvious benefits from government-mandated, universal health programs, why has the United States been incapable of acting?

True, the insurance and health corporations have fogged the picture with bogus propaganda. But that is not the whole story; there are entrenched interests, such as the American Medical Association, that have feared cuts in income or changes in their practice of medicine. Many physicians are now realizing they could fare much worse under the rapidly multiplying restrictions of corporate managed care. But what about the vast number of employers—from big auto manufacturers to fast-food chains to small businesses everywhere—that should have preferred a universal, tax-supported national program over coverage they themselves had to supply?

One suspects that underneath all the discussions of rationing care and the oppressive presence of government there has been an even greater fear among the corporations and the owning classes: that employees with national health service insurance cards in their pockets might feel freer to walk out the door and look for another job, might dare to join in a union-organizing effort, might ask for better working conditions and more respect—all because they wouldn't be afraid of losing their health care benefits. In reality, corporate America is rationing health care right now, through the kind of managed care that the private sector has devised. Only privileged workers get good coverage, many get inadequate insurance, and some get none at all. This allows employers to exert an immense amount of control over their employees. The right to universal health care would allow working people to enjoy a new level of equality and dignity, and from there they could do almost anything.

1. Timothy Smeeding, "America's Income Inequality: Where Do We Stand?," *Challenge*, September–October 1996, p. 50. Anthony B. Atkinson, Lee Rainwater, and Timothy M. Smeeding, *Income Distribution in OECD Countries: The Evidence from the Luxembourg Income Study*, Paris: Organization for Economic Cooperation and Development, 1995.

2. Mishel, Bernstein, and Schmitt, *The State of Working America*, 1996, p. 393. The countries are Australia, Canada, Denmark, France, Germany, Italy, Japan, the Netherlands, Norway, Sweden, Switzerland, and Great Britain. The standard of living is measured according to purchasing power of wages, not the market exchange rates. If market rates were used, many European countries would surpass U.S. wage levels.

3. David Himmelstein and Steffie Woolhandler, *The National Health Program Book*, Monroe, ME: Common Courage Press, 1994, p. 236. Written by two doctors teaching at the Harvard University Medical School, this is a very accessible description of how the U.S. would benefit from a "single-payer" system modeled on the experience of Canada.

4. Ibid., p. 24.

5. Himmelstein and Woolhandler, p. 262.

6. Ibid., p. 264.

7. Ibid., p. 40.

8. Himmelstein and Woolhandler, p. 245.

9. Few citizens ever got to consider the careful description of options provided in a few good reference guides, such as those produced by the League of Women Voters and the Consumers' Union, both of which ultimately recommended a single-payer national health system for the United States.

10. Himmelstein and Woolhandler, p. 191.

11. Leslie Eaton, "Aetna to Buy U.S. Healthcare," *New York Times*, April 2, 1996, p. A1.

12. Dr. Lawrence Miller, quoted in Elisabeth Rosenthal, "Reduced HMO Fees Cause Concern About Patient Care," *New York Times*, November 25, 1996, p. A1.

13. Martin Gottlieb and Kurt Eichenwald, "A Hospital Chain's Brass Knuckles, and the Backlash," *New York Times*, May 11, 1997, Section 3, p. 1.

14. Claire M. Fagin, Letter to the *New York Times*, August 20, 1996.

15. Carl Ginsburg, "The Patient as Profit Center: Hospital Inc. Comes to Town," *The Nation*, November 18, 1996, pp. 18–22.

16. Robert Kuttner, *Everything for Sale*, p. 112.

17. Mark Jaffe, "Talk of price controls a bitter pill for AMA," *Philadelphia Inquirer*, June 20, 1993, pp. D1–3.

18. Himmelstein and Woolhandler, pp. 101–2.

LESSONS FROM THE REST OF THE ADVANCED CAPITALIST WORLD: SOCIAL DEMOCRACY WORKS

For years corporations and the investing class in the United States have been trying to convince the American people that the invisible hand of the global free market requires them to make life leaner and meaner in the workplace. For all the loose talk about the pressures of international competition inevitably forcing wages downward, recent history does not support the theory. Other nations have pursued different outcomes for working people. Germany pays the world's highest wages and still is the world's largest exporter of manufactured goods.

At the end of the 1970s production workers in American manufacturing plants were earning the same amount as their counterparts in Germany. Each country substantially increased its levels of manufacturing productivity in the 1980s, but only the German workers benefited.

CHANGES IN PRODUCTIVITY AND COMPENSATION FROM 1978 TO 1988[1]		
	PRODUCTIVITY	COMPENSATION
United States	up 34%	down 1.5%
Germany	up 32%	up 29%

The German manufacturing workers kept increasing their advantage into the 1990s, and by 1996 were earning 160 percent of the wages and benefits paid to their American counterparts. The U.S. effort to become a low-wage country had no effect on its dismal record in export production. From 1980 to 1995, the U.S. managed to record sixteen straight manufacturing trade deficits with other countries. At the same time other rich nations, which were maintaining high wages and decent standards of benefits and health care for their citizens, were able to sustain strong export economies. Germany, for instance, generated sixteen straight trade surpluses from 1980 through 1996; Japan also racked up sixteen out of sixteen; the Netherlands and Sweden did not do badly, either, with fourteen and thirteen surpluses, respectively, in the same time span.[2]

Perhaps the United States has been playing the wrong game. Elsewhere in the advanced industrialized world, working people retain some power in relation to the owners of capital. This is made manifest in the strength of organized labor.

RATES OF UNIONIZATION IN ADVANCED CAPITALIST COUNTRIES IN THE 1990s[3]	
United States	15%
Japan and France	28%
Canada	36%
Germany	43%
United Kingdom	50%
Denmark and Sweden	96%

This degree of unionization in various workplaces and across all industries definitely promotes political programs that benefit the working class. However, the support for strong social policies and good wages transcends unions and the political parties that support them. In most of Europe it is considered offensive to national pride if industry, with the acquiescence of government, tries to undercut the standard of living achieved by ordinary people. Two major outbursts occurred recently, both under relatively conservative governments, in response to incidents that would be considered the normal course of events in the United States.

In the autumn of 1995, the people of France surprised the conservative government that they had recently elected by supporting a long transportation strike that inconvenienced almost everyone in the country. Middle-class and working-class commuters willingly endured hours of misery locked in traffic jams because they thought that the government was unfairly cutting back on the pay, benefits, and job security of the public transport unions. The solidarity between transport workers and outraged citizens forced the French government to back down; public officials faced humiliation because they had failed to protect a decent working-class standard of living. In the spring of 1997, French voters vented their anger by ousting the conservative prime minister and voting in a legislature that was led by the Socialists.

In the summer of 1996 German employers pressured the conservative Christian Democratic government to limit the generous sick-pay standards that mandated 100 percent pay for up to six weeks of illness. The law passed, allowing reductions to an 80 percent rate, if negotiated with the unions. When big employers tried to put the measures into effect unilaterally, prompting widespread strikes and protests, the government of conservative Prime Minister Helmut Kohl stepped in on the side of the workers. Within a week, several of the biggest corporations in Germany—Daimler Benz, Siemens, and Volkswagen—were forced to back down from their position of not consulting the unions. During the protests, workers carried posters saying, "Don't Treat Us Like Americans!"

Workers Think They Deserve Good Treatment

Working people in Western Europe and Japan have higher expectations than many Americans: they think it is perfectly natural for employers to treat everyone decently. They also earn relatively high wages, having surpassed the pay of U.S. working people over the past twenty years. Ever since 1979, workers in Europe and Japan have been gaining on Americans. One study compared ten countries with the U.S. and showed that those nations' production workers, who had earned 81 cents to every dollar made by Americans in 1979, were earning $1.18 to every American dollar in 1994.[4]

On top of high wages and benefits unheard of in the United States, the workers in other countries also worked fewer hours. In 1995 German manufacturing employees labored about 76 percent of the hours worked by their American counterparts; for the Danish it was 80 percent, for the French 81 percent, and for the Dutch 83 percent. To add insult to injury, the American came up short—very short indeed—on days of paid vacation.

TOTAL PAID DAYS OFF FOR ALL EMPLOYEES[5]	
Germany	30 days vacation plus 12 holidays plus 20 sick days
France	25 days vacation plus 10 holidays plus 19 sick days
U.S.	12 days vacation plus 11 holidays plus 7 sick days

Americans have a difficult time understanding how countries which pay high wages, impose higher taxes, and practice careful intervention in their economies are becoming more prosperous and productive than our own. It also comes as a surprise that these nations do not have nearly as many tiers of management and authority as American business and bureaucracies have. Efficiency and quality of production are enhanced by the low level of supervision:

SUPERVISORY EMPLOYEES AS A PERCENTAGE OF ALL WORKERS[6]			
SWEDEN	GERMANY	JAPAN	UNITED STATES
2.1%	3.9%	4.2%	13%

Economist David M. Gordon has described the differences between "cooperative" and "conflictual" styles of management, particularly contrasting "the carrot" approach used by capitalist firms in Germany, Japan, Sweden, and most of northern Europe as compared to "the stick" approach used in the United States (and, to a lesser extent, in Great Britain and Canada). He noted what ought to be obvious: countries that treat their workers better and offer positive rewards (the carrot) for performance are more productive. Punitive economies, those that practice the "stick" approach, waste far too much labor time on supervisory activity and often underestimate workers' abilities to perform a wide range of tasks independently (not to mention the fact that the pressure of intense management oversight aggravates many workers).

A study by economists Robert Buchele and Jens Christiansen identified the characteristics of countries that offer various "carrots" to their workers and foster "cooperative" relations between management and labor.[7] These societies shared the following advantages over ours:

• greater capital investment in plant and machinery

• higher rates of unionization

• better unemployment benefits

• more provisions for social welfare

• more intensive worker training and continuing education.

The labor-friendly nations that shared all five of these characteristics enjoyed higher productivity growth than ours in the years 1972 to 1988. Their annual rates of increased productivity were:

FRANCE	JAPAN	GERMANY	ITALY
3.4%	3.4%	3.0%	2.8%

The labor-unfriendly nations, with their weak investment in working people, had weaker economic growth. Their annual productivity gains for the same years were:

GREAT BRITAIN	CANADA	UNITED STATES
2.3%	1.7%	0.9%

Productivity growth from 1989 to 1994, a time of severe global recession and slow growth, confirms the same differences: the labor-friendly countries averaged annual productivity rates of 1.6%; the labor-unfriendly group had rates of only 0.8%.[8]

Real economic success in Western Europe and Japan not only goes hand in hand with the maintenance of social protections for working people, but is compatible with high taxes. Nations like Germany and Japan have plenty of rich capitalists, and they tax these citizens at a higher rate because this is considered both economically and socially productive. The maximum tax rate on the rich is over 60 percent in Japan and 53 percent in Germany, far more than the rates of 28 percent to 39.6 percent in the United States (the range between the capital gains and highest income tax rates).

Most of our competitors also levy higher taxes across the board, meaning that their governments have a much larger role in the economy.

TAX REVENUES OF GOVERNMENT AS A PERCENTAGE OF GROSS DOMESTIC PRODUCT[9]					
	U.S.	JAPAN	GERMANY	SWEDEN	FRANCE	NETHERLANDS
1979	28.8%	24.4%	37.8%	49.0%	40.2%	44.3%
1993	29.7%	29.1%	39.0%	49.9%	43.9%	48.0%

These figures give a clear message: government spending does not constitute a drag on economic performance. Growth in productivity and wages were slow in the United States in comparison with other countries even though we kept government spending considerably lower (if military spending were subtracted, our government expenditures would be lower still in relation to others).

Furthermore, in other countries the benefits from increased productivity have been passed along to the people who produce. In 1994 German manufacturing production workers got paid $1.60 for every dollar Americans earned, and workers in other countries did well, too: the Swedish, $1.10; the Dutch, nearly $1.22; the Japanese, $1.25.[10] Of course, their bosses get reasonably compensated, too. But it is not deemed necessary to pay them anywhere near as much as American CEOs, even though they are presiding over operations that work more efficiently. A 1995 study of CEO salaries and bonus compensations at large firms showed that after-tax compensation of American CEOs was 3 to 5 times as great as their counterparts in Germany, Japan, France, and the United Kingdom.

AFTER-TAX PAY OF CEOS IN 1992[11]	
UNITED STATES	EUROPE AND JAPAN
over $500,000	$100,000–$200,000

What About the Lower Classes?

If it is true that the poor will always be with us, then it is also true that societies can radically reduce poverty. Other nations have many fewer people living in poverty than the United States; according to one study of the early 1990s, the contrast in the percentage of children living in poverty was particularly stark:[12]

United States	21.5%
Great Britain	9.9%
Germany	6.8%
France	6.5%
Belgium	3.8%
Sweden	2.7%

An even more important comparison involves what countries do once they take notice of their poor citizens. When countries invest heavily in counteracting the effects of poverty, it becomes possible for people to escape the condition more quickly. A study that followed the experience of poor families with children over a period of three years showed that the transition rate out of poverty can be very fast.

	PERCENTAGE OF ALL FAMILIES WITH CHILDREN WHO ARE POOR FOR ONE YEAR	PERCENTAGE OF ALL FAMILIES WHO REMAIN IN POVERTY FOR THREE YEARS[13]
Germany	4.8%	1.5%
Netherlands	2.7%	0.4%
France	4.0%	1.6%
U.S.	20.0%	14.4%

Yet another dimension of fairness and equality, which helps show why Europeans combat poverty so much more effectively, is revealed in a review of income statistics from Europe. Their lower-income citizens are much better off than ours. Looking at those at the 10th percentile of income (meaning only 10 percent of the population earns less), we see that low-income people in Europe were doing relatively well in the mid-1990s compared with their American counterparts.

FAMILY INCOME AT THE 10TH PERCENTILE AS A PERCENTAGE OF THE MEDIAN INCOME[14]	
France	55%
Germany	57%
Italy	53%
Sweden	55%
U.S.	35%

The Threat of American-Style, Globalizing Capitalism

All is not rosy, however, in the more humane societies of Europe and Japan. The "welfare states" created by social democracy are being undermined as the rest of the world shifts toward marketization of every human activity. Many nations, particularly in East Asia, are helping to maximize corporate profits by imposing authoritarian management and austerity. The biggest single problem in Europe is unemployment, which hovered around 10 percent for most European countries in the mid–1990s. However, because Europeans use stricter criteria for measuring unemployment than the United States, the American claim that we have only half as high an unemployment rate should be taken with a grain of salt. Economist Jeff Faux found that the German unemployment rate of 1996 was 7.2 percent (rather than over 10 percent), if he used the looser methods of the U.S. government (which showed our unemployment to be 5.4 percent).[15]

Still, the threat posed by unemployment to the stability of European societies is very real. European working people are worried about becoming redundant in the worldwide scheme of production, threatened not so much by U.S. competition as by the goods produced for a fraction of the cost by exploited labor in developing countries. The left-leaning parties of Europe and their labor union allies would like to protect themselves within the fortress of the European Union. To a certain extent they can do that, especially through efforts to keep wages and benefits high while employing more people by providing for a shorter workweek. The French government announced plans in 1997 to start introducing a "full" workweek of thirty-five hours or less. In the Netherlands working people are concerned about the intrusion of U.S.-style contingent labor and part-time work; the danger of losing permanent jobs is real, but so far the Dutch unions have been largely successful in demanding full-scale wages and benefits for these new classes of temporary employees.

The greatest danger to working people in Europe is posed by their own financiers and capitalists, who are tempted to disinvest in their own economies because they smell higher returns on their money elsewhere. An instructive lesson was provided by Sweden in the 1990s. After 1989, when Swedish financiers pushed the government to lift foreign exchange controls, there was a tremen-

dous flight of capital as major Swedish transnational companies and banks rapidly pursued production opportunities in other countries. The old cooperative relationship with labor was, in the words of Stuart Wilks, "rejected by a domestic industrial sector which needed to develop more flexible production and investment strategies in a globalized economic system."[16] The social democratic government was pushed out of power in 1991 because unemployment jumped to 3.5 percent, but the new conservative government was worse; its failure to control currency and speculation led to a "fiasco," according to economist Helen Lachs Ginsburg, which "converted a recession into a depression marked by three years of declining output, the loss of one-tenth of Sweden's jobs, and record unemployment" of over 10 percent.[17] Social Democrats came back into their customary position in power in 1994, but in a much weaker position.

The populations of all advanced capitalist countries face similar threats. Those who have enjoyed the advantages of social democratic life on a national level for fifty years will have to consider taking new risks, but this should not mean allowing the global free market to exploit them. Europeans may have to go beyond the boundaries of fortress Europe, risking a progressive counter-offensive that commits them, the working people of the "North," to fight for better pay and more freedom for working people in the rapidly industrializing "South." If they do not keep up with the scramble of international capital, the humanizing values of social democracy may not survive.

1. U.S. Department of Labor, *Handbook of Labor Statistics*, 1989, pp. 561 and 576.

2. Barlett and Steele, *America: Who Stole the Dream?*, p. 46.

3. M. E. Sharpe, "Labor's Future," *Challenge*, March–April 1996, p. 66.

4. Bureau of Labor Standards data as shown by Mishel, Bernstein, and Schmitt, 1996, p. 392.

Japan made the biggest overall gains, with pay going from $.60 in 1979 to $1.25 in 1996.

5. Roger Cohen, "Europeans Consider Shortening Workweek to Relieve Joblessness," *New York Times*, November 22, 1993, p. A6.

6. David M. Gordon, *Fat and Mean*, p. 47. Gordon, renowned for his economic analysis of workplace efficiency and the deleterious effects of top-heavy management, used these figures from 1989 as being the best available as of 1996. If anything, he reported, preliminary analysis in the mid-1990s was showing that the U.S. position in relation to other countries was getting worse. Corporate downsizing, for all the talk of trimming management, was actually doing the reverse: the ratio of supervisors to workers was getting even higher, rather than lower, than the 1989 figure of 13 percent.

7. Robert Buchele and Jens Christiansen, "Workers' Rights Promote Productivity," *Challenge*, September–October 1995.

8. The figures for 1989–94 were outside the scope of the Buchele-Christiansen study and come from the international comparisons found in Mishel, Bernstein, and Schmitt, *The State of Working America*, p. 384.

9. Mishel, Bernstein, and Schmitt, 1996, p. 103.

10. Mishel and Bernstein, 1994, p. 338, comparative wages for 1992. These are market wages, which are more useful for discussions that involve manufacturing productivity because they may affect the competitiveness of exports. However, they can change as the values of currencies change.

11. J. M. Abowd and M. L. Bognanno, "International Differences in Executive and Managerial Compensation," in R. Freeman and L. Katz (eds.), *Differences and Changes in Wage Structure*, Chicago: University of Chicago Press, 1995. American CEO compensation is lower in this comparison than in the *Business Week* figures given earlier, because this study includes more managers from smaller companies, as well as the Fortune 500.

12. Lee Rainwater and Timothy M. Smeeding, "Doing Poorly: the Real Income of American Children in a Comparative Perspective," Working Paper No. 127. Syracuse, N.Y.: The Maxwell School, Syracuse University, 1995.

13. Gregg Duncan, et al., "Poverty and Social Assistance Dynamics in the United States, Canada, and Europe," paper presented at the Poverty and Public Policy conference, Washington, D.C., 1991.

14. Anthony Atkinson, Lee Rainwater, and Timothy M. Smeeding, *Income Distribution in OECD Countries: Evidence from the Luxembourg Income Study*, Paris: Organization for Economic Cooperation and Development, 1995.

15. Jeff Faux, "The 'American' Model Exposed," *The Nation*, October 27, 1997, p. 18.

16. Stuart Wilks, "Class Compromise and the International Economy: The Rise and Fall of Swedish Social Democracy," *Capital & Class*, Spring 1996, pp. 107-8. Two positive interpretations of social democracy in Sweden: Henry Milner, *Sweden: Social Democracy in Practice*, New York: Oxford University Press, 1989; Michael Harrington, *Socialism: Past and Future*, New York: Little, Brown, 1989.

17. Helen Lachs Ginsburg, "Fall from Grace," *In These Times*, December 23, 1995.

OUR
COUNTRY IS
SO RICH

Unless you redistribute the wealth of a country into the hands of the people every fifty years, your country's got to go to ruination.

—HUEY LONG,
Governor of Louisiana, 1932[1]

Despite our deficits, our humiliating treatment of the poor, and our awe of the wealthy, the United States is still the richest nation in the world. We can easily afford to have a country with no poor people, if we so choose.

There is enough money in our economy to eliminate poverty altogether. Without being particularly egalitarian, we could have provided a decent job for each person who wanted one in 1996, and everyone's income would have been far above the official poverty line of $15,150 for a family of four. For example:

SUGGESTED ANNUAL INCOMES FOR 133 MILLION WORKING AMERICANS[2]				
YOUNG AND PART-TIME WORKERS (15%)	LOWER-LEVEL WORKERS (15%)	MIDDLE-RANGE WORKERS (60%)	SPECIAL PROFESSIONS, MANAGERS (9%)	HIGHEST MANAGERS, OWNERS (1%)
$20,000	$30,000	$45,000	$90,000	$200,000[3]

It is not necessary to propose an absolute leveling of income in order to provide a job and an adequate standard of living for everyone. As the figures above demonstrate, we can allow differentials in earnings that are wide enough to provide rewards for experience and skill and incentives for effort and advancement.

Is such a proposal impossibly utopian? Is it naive to expect that societies could arrange themselves in such a way?

The ancient Greeks thought that excess wealth, much of it produced by slaves, was a problem in their democracy. Plato wrote in *The Laws* that the richest citizen ought to own about four times as much as the poorest. Aristotle gave more leeway, but not much: he thought a five-to-one ratio was appropriate.[4]

In the twentieth century there are democracies that allow all working people to participate fully as citizens and also provide some measure of equitable distribution among them. As shown in chapter 18, the distribution of income in Europe and Japan now approaches or betters the ratios favored by the ancient Greeks; that is, the ratio of high family earnings to low family earnings is in the range of 3 to 1 or 4 to 1. A tiny set of capitalists, of course, exists outside of this part of the bargain. But democratic forces fighting from below have been able to compel the very rich to pay high taxes and maintain decent wages for the majority.

As it turns out, the calculation of "suggested incomes for 133 million working Americans" that appears on the previous page is not utopian at all.[5] It merely applies the European ratios of high incomes to low incomes to the United States, so that no one works for poverty wages and most people are well paid. Moreover, when we consider the number of two-earner households, we have the means to provide a very comfortable life for most Americans.

What Is Fair, Here and There?

We have established that it is possible for Americans to enjoy the kind of income distribution that exists in Europe. But what about the social acceptability of asking for a fairer society? Americans have become accustomed to think that their society is made up of winners and losers, and a great many working people have come to accept their place among the losers.

Two American researchers, Sidney Verba and Robert R. Orren, conducted an interesting study of the standards of fairness in the United States and Sweden in the 1980s. Sweden is a place where social democratic notions of equality and "economic democracy" have infused all sectors of society, so it is ideal for comparison with the United States, where a strong capitalist point of view is purveyed to all social classes by the corporate media. The researchers found that the two countries displayed radically different ideas of how much a person's labor is worth. This was evident when workers and executives in both countries were asked what they considered a fair difference in pay between top executives and the lowest-paid employees.

- U.S. executives thought they should be paid about 26 times more than the lowliest workers.

- U.S. workers did not agree but still accepted a pay ratio of 11.3 to 1 as fair.

- Swedish executives felt they deserved only 4.7 times as much as workers at the bottom.

- Swedish workers, while not perfectly egalitarian in philosophy, certainly didn't want the bosses getting rich at their expense: they favored a pay differential of 2.2 to 1.

We should note that in each case the bosses thought pay should be more unequal than their workers did. But the Swedish bosses accepted a level of equality that Americans didn't dare dream about. This does not mean that Swedish executives were especially sympathetic to workers; just as their American counterparts do, they band together in associations of manufacturers to oppose workers' and unions' demands. Rather, it suggests that the consciousness promoted by years of social democracy has filtered into the minds of all Swedish citizens, rich and poor alike. Hence we have a rather remarkable situation, as defined by Sidney Verba and Gary R. Owen (*Equality in America*, Harvard University Press, 1985): "Swedish business leaders are sharply more egalitarian than any group in the United States, including left-liberals."

How Do Ordinary Citizens Find a Voice in Politics?

Americans are not necessarily opposed to building a more equal society, but their politicians seldom give them the option. Polls of the American public over the past twenty years have repeatedly showed that a large majority favors a government that provides full employment at decent wages, good health care for all, adequate housing, a healthy environment, and a host of other "progressive" programs.[6] These ideas had a lot of popular appeal, but big money did not support them, and they never became law.

But it need not have been so. Most Americans were at least partly aware of increasing social inequalities and might well have responded to the Democratic Party if it had proposed progressive economic solutions. But Clinton and the Democratic Leadership Council were too busy trying to reshape the Democrats into a moderate conservative party

that could match Republican attractiveness to big business. The Democratic National Committee (DNC) even advertised the following deal—contributors of $100,000 or more to Clinton's reelection fund would receive: two dinners with President Clinton, two dinners with Vice President Al Gore, a seat on the administration plane going on the foreign trade mission of their choice, and daily fax reports from a staff member of the DNC.

In such an atmosphere one might think that both the Democrats and Republicans had fooled the common people into believing in an ideology that serves only the elite. But this was not the case. In what may have been the most interesting poll conducted before the 1996 election, the viewpoints of one thousand ordinary citizens were compared with those of two hundred big-money contributors, half of whom supported the Democratic Party, half the Republicans.[7] While the Democratic contributors were more liberal than the Republicans, they were both at odds with the nonrich electorate on some very significant issues:

- Of the ordinary citizens, 83 percent believed: "Average working families have less economic security today, because corporations have become too greedy and care more about their profits than about being fair and loyal to their employees."

A majority of the big contributors disagreed.

- Almost 66 percent of the big donors believed that "government spends too much and interferes in things better left to individuals and business."

A majority of citizens disagreed.

- Most Americans saw free-trade agreements such as NAFTA as job losers rather than job creators, by 59 to 25 percent.

The big pockets, Democrats even more than Republicans, thought that free-trade deals were creating jobs, by 65 to 24 percent. (According to all data, they are wrong.)

• Ordinary citizens were not so worried about big, bad government. In fact, by a margin of 53 to 38, they agreed that "we need to make government regulations tougher in order to stop companies from moving jobs overseas, polluting here at home, and treating their workers badly."

• The moneybags said "government regulations go too far," by 55 to 31 percent.

The political program presented by both parties in 1996 more or less matched the opinions of the elite donors. Perhaps the Democratic leadership had fooled itself into believing that what the common people wanted was the same as what its biggest campaign contributors wanted.

Meanwhile, the right-wing pseudopopulism and bigotry that Ronald Reagan and George Bush had so cleverly encouraged were still very much alive. For years white working people had been distracted from the fact that the rich were successfully waging class warfare against them. The antiwelfare rhetoric of 1996, voiced by Republicans and echoed by Clinton, only helped to stoke the suspicions and frustrations of white Americans who feared for their futures. Political analyst Ruy Teixeira pointed out that white men did have something to be angry about; many of them had in fact suffered steep declines in wages. Unfortunately, the right-wing talk shows encouraged disgruntled males to blame the usual villains—ethnic and racial minorities, as well as women— rather than think about why they and others were being forced to take jobs for less money.

What Would They Want If They Showed Up To Vote?

American voters seem to have realized that there is less and less for them to vote for. As the Democratic Party turns into a faint imitation of the Republicans, more people stay home from the polls. The portion of eligible people who vote in presidential elections has steadily fallen: 61–63 percent in the 1960s; 53–55 percent in the 1970s; 50–53 percent in the 1980s; and, after a brief upturn to 55 percent when Ross Perot appeared as a third candidate in 1992, 49 percent in 1996. The reelection of Bill Clinton was hardly an endorsement of anything, because he received only 45 million votes out of 187 million eligible voters (24 percent of the potential electorate). His Republican opponent's 38 million votes (only 20 percent of those eligible) might have seemed pathetic, except for the fact that whatever the outcome, the country was still under the sway of a conservative agenda that Bob Dole would be happy to claim as his own.

Today the working and middle classes of Europe are battling at the polls to keep the social and economic gains they earned over the past fifty years. In recent decades voter turnout in France has averaged 77 percent; in the Netherlands, 82 percent; in Germany, 84 percent; in Sweden, 87 percent; and in Italy, 93 percent. The "left" in Europe has become very moderate—some would say it has ended up in the center—but citizens there still feel they have something to vote for.

So what about that 51 percent of the American electorate, those 95 million people who did not vote in the last presidential election? How would their votes have affected our political outcomes if they had something to vote for? We cannot be sure, but we can make some guesses based on the profiles of those who didn't vote. They are overwhelmingly people with less than four years of college who have low and modest incomes. This means they come from the working-class majority, the three quarters of our population that did not attend or finish college. Voting rates among this segment of the population are about 40 percent. Compare this with the rate among college graduates (25 percent of the population) and those who earned over $75,000 per year (8 percent of the population): the latter two groups turn out to vote at a rate exceeding 80 percent.

Bill Clinton was clearly not speaking to the working class when he courted suburbanites with his carefully crafted moderate conservatism. But the working class wanted the same things that appealed to the "soccer moms": decent pay for their work, safe neighborhoods, good day care for their children, and guaranteed health care. Disgruntled males in the working class had reason to be disturbed about the state of affairs in 1996, but they did not take the racial or gender bait dangled by the Republicans. Male high school graduates (with no college) voted 46 percent for Clinton and only 36 percent for Dole, almost as wide a margin as existed among suburban women; other women, the noncollege grads from the working class, voted for Clinton even more decisively than did the soccer moms.

Even though the Democratic leadership has been so indifferent to workers and the poor in recent years, most working people who vote still feel they have nowhere else to go:

PERCENTAGE OF PEOPLE WHO VOTED FOR CLINTON AGAINST DOLE	INCOME GROUP
59 to 28%	Under $15,000
53 to 36%	$15,000–$30,000
41 to 51%	Over $75,000
38 to 54%	Over $100,000

In congressional elections, the extreme differences between rich and poor are just as great: those who earn over $100,000 vote Republican 63 to 37 percent and those who earn under $15,000 go for Democrats by exactly the same margin. The only other self-identified group which voted in such a partisan fashion is the "white Christian right," which went for Republicans by a margin of 73 to 27 percent.

But suppose the Democrats decided to throw off their clumsy disguise as a second Republican Party and tried to offer a fresh version of the New Deal, in the process throwing in Harry Truman's fifty-year-old plan to provide universal health care. What if Americans were offered the kind of income equality that exists in Europe, which would make the "Suggested Annual Incomes" listed at the beginning of this chapter a real possibility? Then the bottom three quarters of the population would have something to vote for, just like the people who flock to the polls in Europe. If working people had gone to the polls at the 80 percent rate of the college graduates and the wealthy, and if they had cast 60 percent of their votes for Clinton (as did other people in their economic circumstances), Clinton could have had a Democratic Congress and gained an additional 11-million-vote advantage over Dole at the same time.[8]

Only a progressive populism that offers universal benefits to all Americans can triumph over the misconceived and divisive politics built on class, race, and gender prejudices. If there is a way to attract a large majority of Americans to a fresh social vision, it will require that the Democratic Party reformulate itself into something much more democratic. On the other hand, if the Democrats proceed with their reformulation into clones of the Republicans, working Americans will have to construct a new political party.

1. Carleton Beales, *The Story of Huey Long*, Westport: Greenwood Press, 1935, p. 245. Huey Long, now remembered only as a political demagogue, was the product of the Populist tradition that was still strong in the poor parishes of Louisiana. His "Share the Wealth" clubs, which were set up around the United States in the 1930s, claimed over 7 million members. Carleton Beales was a journalist who was critical of Long. Nevertheless he wrote that the clubs "represented the largest active political organization ever put together in this country." Some historians have credited Long (who had hoped to run for president in 1936, but was assassinated the year before) with contributing to the working-class pressure that pushed Franklin Roosevelt and the Democratic Party toward egalitarian reforms in the mid-1930s.

2. In order to make sure everyone is productively employed, a shorter workweek is in order. Suggested incomes are based on a 1,600-hour work year (average 32 hours × 50 weeks). Low pay = $12.50 per hour; low middle = $18.75; middle pay = $28 per hour; high pay = $56 per hour; top managers and owners, $150 per hour.

3. Barlett and Steele (1996, p. xi) report that in 1993, 45 percent of American tax returns were filed for incomes under $20,000, 47 percent for incomes between $20,000 and $75,000, and 8 percent for incomes over $75,000; the top 1 percent averaged $464,800. Each IRS income level is a bit low due to underreporting. However, experts on taxes and income say that the rich underreport their income the most, as much as 50 percent on property income. Since most people's wages are reported on W-2 forms, they have no such opportunity.

4. Henry Phelps Brown, *Egalitarianism and the Generation of Inequality*, Oxford: Clarendon Press, 1988, p. 139.

5. Personal income in 1996 was about $6.5 trillion. If 133 million working Americans—all those who were employed, self-employed, and unemployed in 1996—had divided up that income (after providing for the elderly), each person would have earned approximately $45,000 a year.

6. If we look back to the 1980s, we find that people favored most of this progressive program even at the height of Ronald Reagan's popularity:

- 21 percent of Americans in 1986 thought government was spending too much on environmental, health, education, welfare, and urban programs, but 41% thought it was spending too little.

- 71 percent preferred military spending cuts to cuts in education; 67 percent wanted to cut military spending instead of health expenditures.

- 74 percent supported a public jobs program even if it meant increasing the size of the federal deficit.

- 5 percent thought federal regulations on safety, consumer protection, and the environment were too strict, but 42 percent thought they weren't strict enough. The four survey results above come from the following sources: National Public Research Center, 1980; Harris Survey, 1984; CBS–*New York Times* poll, 1983; *Los Angeles Times*, 1982.

7. Robert L. Borosage and Ruy Teixeira, "The Politics of Money," *The Nation*, October 21, 1996, p. 21. The data that follow came from polls conducted by Lake Research in July 1996 for *The Nation* and the Institute for America's Future.

8. These calculations are necessarily crude, but the differences are so starkly obvious that there is no mistaking the fact that upper-income people vote at twice the rate, at least, of lower-income groups. Exit polls depend on the veracity and accuracy of the interviewee: there are bound to be discrepancies when data about income and education are compared with census and IRS data. The Voter News Service provided the data on almost seventeen thousand voters at three hundred polling places around the nation. College-graduate males cast 46 percent of the male votes in 1996, even though they only make up 25 percent of the male population; they turned out at a rate of 88 percent, compared with about 35 per-

cent for the rest of American men. College-graduate females cast 41 percent of the female vote while making up 25 percent of the population, meaning they turned out at 84 percent compared with 40 percent for the rest of American women. Similarly, those who earn over $75,000 per year make up 8 percent to 10 percent of the population, but account for 18 percent of the voter turnout. These figures were for a presidential election; in off-year congressional races, when overall turnout is much lower, the college-educated, higher-income, suburbanite voters represent an even larger part of the electorate. In 1996, for instance, 39 percent of the voters who turned out lived in suburbs, but in 1994, 48 percent were suburbanites.

IF WE DECIDED

TO TAX

THE RICH

The very rich are different from you and me.
—F. SCOTT FITZGERALD

Yes . . . they have more money.
—ERNEST HEMINGWAY

Can the people of the United States retake control, once again taxing the richest citizens at a progressive rate and creating a fair society for all? If we had a Congress and a president who were willing to promote the interests of the vast majority of Americans, we could recapture some of the accumulated wealth that has been transferred to the rich over the last two decades. A reallocation of our resources could serve working people in the following ways:

• by creating full employment, with a higher minimum wage and shorter workweek[1]

• by supporting quality day care for all who need it[2]

• by providing for federally funded health care that serves everyone

• by rebuilding the nation's schools, roads, bridges, sewers, and parks

• by offering free higher education and other training to all citizens

Measures such as this will certainly cost hundreds of billions of dollars. Where can we get this kind of money while keeping the budget deficit reasonably low? There are several places to start:

• We must reestablish upper-bracket federal income tax rates comparable to those imposed during the prosperous decades of the 1950s and 1960s. The current effective rate on the richest 1 percent, whose income is at least $900 billion per year, is about 25 percent. An effective tax rate of 50 percent on the very richest 1 percent of Americans would raise an extra $225 billion.[3]

• Raise the effective tax rate on corporate profits to 50 percent, the approximate rate of the 1950s. Profits have risen dramatically, to over $600 billion per year, while taxes have remained at an effective rate of about 25 percent, so this increase would yield another $150 billion.

• Institute an annual wealth tax of 3 percent on the richest 1 percent of Americans; this will yield $250 billion per year.[4]

• Cut defense spending on new weaponry by $100 billion to stay in line with the diminished military budgets of the rest of the world.[5]

These proposals, and the $725 billion they would raise, might outrage the corporations and the rich, as well as the politicians whom they have so carefully cultivated; but it would hardly be a case of impoverishing the well-to-do. The $625 billion in increased taxation would simply restore the more equitable (but hardly equal) distribution of income and wealth enjoyed by Americans three decades ago. The exact fiscal measures used to achieve more egalitarian economic outcomes are not all that important; the ones listed above could be modified or par-

tially replaced by others. (For instance, Social Security taxes could be made less regressive by assessing them on the highest salaries, and on all forms of property and financial income as well.[6] Other worthy forms of taxation could be reestablished, such as the once progressive but now largely eviscerated inheritance tax.)

Big Problems Require Big Solutions

A class war, waged by the rich with very little opposition from the working class, has already taken place. The size of economic transfers recommended here would enable us to redress the imbalance of power in appropriate proportion to the inequality that has been imposed over the past twenty years.[7] The money is there, and its redistribution back to working people would establish the balance that exists in most of the other highly industrialized countries.

Righting the imbalance between the rich and the working class is not just a matter of tinkering with budget deficit rules or massaging the Consumer Price Index or the measures of productivity.[8] It is a battle for political and economic power, a matter of control over the political economy. Sharing our economic resources more equitably again will require ordinary citizens to exercise their democratic rights in a determined and unified manner. This fundamental shift cannot be accomplished by a quick swing of voters in one election, but only through a lengthy process of education and organization that convinces the American people that major changes are both desirable and possible.

Labor and Work

Even though labor unions in the United States threw $35 million into targeted congressional races in 1996, there is little merit in the conservative claim that organized labor has the same kind of power in the Democratic Party as big business interests have in the Republican Party. Unions have resources that are minuscule compared with those of business interests: in 1996, all labor associations together collected $6 billion in dues, as compared with the $4 trillion in revenues and $360 billion in profits gathered by corporations. Labor can gain politically only when millions of working people, unionized and nonunionized, are engaged in the political process.

There are reasons for optimism. Despite the fact that the percentage of organized workers has been more than cut in half in the past forty years, from 35 percent to less than 15 percent, unions have made recent gains in organizing women, Hispanics, and African-Americans as members. In making an effort to organize the working poor and to alleviate the exploitation of part-time and contingent workers, unions are reviving the universal goals that once gave life to the labor movement. The emphasis on raising the wages of those at the bottom is crucial in two ways: it stresses the equal status due to all those who are willing to work, and it protects the wages and benefits of those already organized.

A distinct turnaround in public perceptions of the labor movement became evident in August of 1997 during the strike by drivers and package handlers at United Parcel Service. Opinion polls showed that Americans backed the Teamsters over UPS management by a margin of 2 to 1. This was a bit surprising given the Teamsters' well-publicized history of corruption and the fact that UPS was generally regarded as a good company. Two beliefs seemed most compelling to average Americans: first, that a company making billions in profits should be able to share them with hardworking employees; and second, that a company which had increased its number of part-timers to over 60 percent of its workforce, then paid them only half the wages of full-time workers, was trying to screw people over. This resonated with many average Americans who had either experienced downsizing themselves or who clearly understood that many companies felt free to throw loyal and competent workers aside.

The shift in public attitudes was having an effect on some voices emanating from the business press. *Business Week*, which had celebrated corporate CEOs as "stars" who deserved the 30 percent raises they received in 1995, did an about-face in April of 1997 when it reviewed the 54 percent increase in CEO compensation for 1996: "Call it Executive Over-Compensation," read the headline of their editorial, which concluded, "Compensation is running riot in many corner offices of corporate America. This simply has to stop."[9] More surprising still was the magazine's reaction when it uncovered a tiny increase in wages of working Americans (about 1 percent) that had occurred between the summer of 1996 and the summer of 1997: "The prosperity of recent years is finally being shared by those in the lower tier of the economy—and that is cause for celebration, not despair." While *Business Week* was obviously premature in announcing that prosperity was being shared, its sentiments suggested that American concerns with inequality were finally being heard.

While the destruction of the social safety net has been a defeat for labor, welfare itself can be redefined by a progressive, labor-backed political program. Welfare should represent part of a universal social contract that can be extended to anyone who meets with severe economic hardships. The contract would make only one demand: that every capable citizen be willing to work. In return each citizen would receive good wages, quality education, and job training, with the added benefits of universal health care and day care. This kind of practical social democracy, grounded in the culture of working people, would quickly deflate the false claims of the right, that the poor are "lazy," "shiftless," and worse. The vast majority of the unemployed and underemployed poor, of whatever race, would be happy to claim membership in a newly dignified working class.

The power of labor has been unfairly curtailed in recent decades, so it is necessary to fight the legal restrictions and management policies that prevent union activity among the poorly paid and unorganized. But this alone is not sufficient. The more challenging task is convincing a good portion of the middle class that it too benefits from working-class mobilization. New kinds of political and social organizations must be formed—not necessarily traditional labor unions—to articulate the goals that middle-class employees share with lower-paid workers. Political solutions will require a very broad solidarity among working Americans, a solidarity that can bridge class, racial, and ethnic lines. This should not be too difficult at a time when working conditions, benefits, and job security are deteriorating even among privileged salaried workers, and when many in the so-called middle class are being subjected to "working-class" treatment by senior management.

Conclusion

This short book is filled with facts and numbers and analyses that some will consider negative, depressing, and downright un-American. My purpose in drawing this picture of the political economy is to plant the seeds of understanding in the minds of working Americans. Not all of our economic and social problems began in the last two decades of the twentieth century, but the policies pursued during the Reagan-Bush-Clinton era have made things considerably worse. Working people have suffered so that a small elite could enlarge its fortunes. In turn, this accumulated money has been wasted on speculative trading, widespread fraud, and nonproductive sectors of the economy, as well as corporate investment in countries where labor is provided by desperately poor people.

The old structures of capital accumulation have brought us regular cycles of poverty and depression in the past. Today things are worse, for capital has lost whatever productive drive and capability it once possessed; the glorification of entrepreneurship in the 1980s brought on the destruction, not the multiplication, of our national assets. The upper class tried to regenerate itself through money games that were far removed from real economic production: the plunder of the banking system, the privatization of public savings, and the paper trade in corporate assets.

It seemed, only a few years back, that if the United States failed to break these habits we would keep sinking in relation to other highly industrialized countries. The ascent of the economies of Japan, Germany, and the rest of Western Europe from 1950 to 1990 was remarkable. They seemed poised to leave us behind precisely because they were taking much better care of their people at the same time that their societies were becoming more productive.

Today something more frightening is happening. The United States, in concert with the corporate engines of globalization, may well bring the rest of the industrialized world down to its level. Once that has happened, the forces unleashed by international finance capital will keep pushing living standards downward. It is uncertain whether the kinds of social democracy set up in Western Europe can survive the current trends that have internationalized capital. Now, as capital moves quickly from continent to continent, often searching for cheap labor disciplined by authoritarian regimes, the capitalists are becoming more internationalized, too (whether they know it or not). They cannot possibly show loyalty, whether feigned or real, to the working and middle classes in their own countries.

Without a sharp turnaround toward democracy and equality in the United States, Europe will be virtually alone in its commitment to social democracy. The pressures of low-wage immigrant labor, cheap imports from Eastern Europe and Asia, and free-market practices of governments are already threatening once secure areas of employment and causing right-wing populism to pop up in various Western European countries. Surprising numbers of middle-class and working-class voters have supported ultranationalist, neofascist parties throughout Europe because, like white male workers in the United States, they see their status slipping.

Europe's weakened remnants of social democracy may survive for a while, but are unlikely to do very well if the American, Japanese, and other international investors (including Europeans) keep filling the world's markets with cheaper products produced by mainland Chinese, Indonesians, Thais, Vietnamese, Filipinos, and others in the vast new workhouse of Asia. In this chaotic world mess, the authoritarian/austerity regimes based on the Taiwanese and South Korean experience will be the model for modern development; their kinds of management teams are exportable, as are their long hours and brutal working conditions. These factors are rapidly turning China, the ultimate labor resource, into a giant replica of the Asian Tiger economy.

In the United States few mainstream commentators are paying attention to the ways that "free-trade" ideology is undermining real freedom. They have failed, for instance, to see the dark portents behind President Clinton's willingness to seek campaign contributions from Indonesian billionaires and Chinese corporations. Conservative columnist and former Nixon speechwriter William Safire was one of the few to see the situation clearly when he described "the central point of the ideo-economic struggle going on in today's world. On one side are governments that put 'order' above all, and offer an under-the-table partnership to managers who like arranged outcomes and a docile work force."

If Arkansas, which looks suspiciously like a center of third world development within the United States, is the economic and political model stuck inside our President's head, then we are already in trouble. And if Singapore is the model state for globalizing high-tech development in the eyes of the world's investing class, then we are drifting toward something worse: an illusion of democracy called "authoritarian democracy."

Nearly one hundred and seventy years ago, Alexis de Tocqueville wrote that "the manufacturing aristocracy which is growing up before our eyes is one of the harshest that ever existed in the world. . . . If ever a permanent inequality of conditions and aristocracy again penetrate the world, it may be predicted that this is the gate by which they will enter." The new corporate aristocracy—controlling not just transnational manufacturing but also worldwide finance and services—is more powerful than anything de Tocqueville could have imagined, and it has diminished the prospects for democracy in America.

The citizens of the United States need to restrain the single-minded accumulation of private capital, invest in strong public institutions, and give human values some room to thrive. Real democracy requires that the people find ways to share wealth and power.

As the repositories of immense wealth and technical expertise, the rich nations of the North ought to promote peaceful and fair development rather than unleash free-market chaos throughout the rest of the world. At home, the productive forces of the United States and the other advanced industrialized countries are easily sufficient to enhance equality and democratic values, as well as provide a comfortable standard of living for all.

1. Shorten the workweek to between 32 and 35 hours and pay a nonpoverty minimum wage. France's minimum wage was about $8 in 1994; British Columbia's was about $7.50 in 1996.

2. Spend $50 billion per year, $5,000 a year per child, to support quality day care for 10 million children, regardless of the income of their parents. Also, provide $2,000 per year per child, for up to two children, to all parents regardless of income. This will cost about $120 billion, but could be paid for by eliminating all personal deductions for adults and all mortgage deductions for home owners. The German government paid all families $135 to $200 per month per offspring in 1996 to help with the costs of child-rearing.

3. Based on total personal income of $6.5 trillion for 1996 × 14 percent share for the top 1 percent × 50 percent = $455 billion. This income share for the very rich might be conservative; Wolff (1996) estimated a 15.7 percent share for 1992, based on the last Federal Reserve data available.

4. Based on wealth of the richest 1 percent measured by Wolff (1996) for 1989, about $8.3 trillion. The $250 billion figure is probably a conservative one, because after falling to $7.5 trillion following the recession of 1990–91, the wealth of the rich should now be $10–$12 trillion, given the long run-up in stock prices. There are more drastic measures, such as the Swedish tax on wealth, which is levied on all wealth from $56,000 to $200,000 at 1.5 percent to 2 percent, and on everything over $200,000 at 3 percent. Edward N. Wolff (1996) estimates that such a tax would yield $330 billion per year, or about 74 percent of what is raised by individual income taxes.

5. Unnecessary weapons programs constitute another kind of AFDC: Aid to Frantically Dependent Corporations.

6. This could either lower the rate of withholding taxes drastically, by about one half for average working people, or increase revenues substantially. At the 1996 rate, FICA taxes would raise $800 billion, instead of $400 billion, if applied to all income. This would also be a convenient way to fund universal health insurance.

7. There can be a problem, both politically and economically, with being too modest. Wolff (1996, p. 57) suggested a wealth tax modeled on the one in Switzerland (believe it or not, that country of practical bankers raises substantial revenues by taxing wealth directly). But the small scale proposed, taxing wealth at 0.3 percent, neither raises enough revenue (only $40 billion per year) nor is large enough to reestablish more balance between the working and middle classes and the rich. Phillips (1994, p. 267), after listing a number of kinds of tax increases that should and could be levied against the very wealthy—more progressive income taxes, capital gains taxes, wealth taxes, and inheritance taxes—then falls back to recommending the extremely modest sum of $40 billion in extra revenue. These are mere symbolic gestures, as Phillips readily admits: "The symbolism of once again demanding more from the rich, pursued in moderation, could have a surprise element of national renewal."

8. See Paul R. Krugman, "New Math, Same Story", *New York Times Magazine*, January 5, 1997, pp. 32–33, for a sharp dissection of new conservative arguments concerning the rates of inflation and productivity increase. Basically he shows

that they are indulging in a statistical game to try to make the dismal economic performance of the past two decades look better in historical terms. True, if the CPI calculations are changed enough, the decline in worker incomes will not look so bad. Except that, argues Krugman, these calculations must then also be applied to the decades of the 1950s through the 1980s, which will raise the performance levels there, too. In the end, that era will always be shown to outperform the Reagan-Bush-Clinton-Greenspan era by a very wide margin. Dean Baker of the Economic Policy Instiitute has also done a good job of countering the not very convincing arguments that "it's the CPI's fault." No matter which way the figures are massaged, the stark differences between high-paid execs and low-paid workers will remain.

9. Even independent, professional members of the middle class are feeling the squeeze. A recent *Business Week* editorial (April 21, 1997) announced that podiatrists are organizing a union to serve their ranks, fourteen thousand foot doctors across the country, and help them do battle with the HMOs.

WHERE TO GO FROM HERE

Since the original *Sharing the Pie* was published in 1988, a number of good books have been published which deal with various aspects of America's economic decline and its increase in economic inequality. Because *Sharing the Pie* offers a broad view of the American political economy, it does not supply in-depth analysis on many subjects; the following books and authors are recommended because they offer extensive data and discussion on various economic themes.

RECOMMENDED READING

Lawrence Mishel, Jared Bernstein, and John Schmitt, *The State of Working America, 1996–97*, Armonk, NY: M. E. Sharpe, 1997: the best collection of statistical analysis of economic trends as they affect American workers and families. Although the authors' perspective is liberal, they have gone to extreme pains to patiently consider, analyze, and rebut the conservative explanations for growing inequality. The business press often relies on analysis from *Working America* because there is no conservative counterpart of equal breadth and depth. The economic views of most conservative thinkers are funded and applauded by the conservative business community in the U.S.; thus these pundits often serve as cheerleaders for the status quo rather than engaging in the kind of sharp and sophisticated analysis found in *The State of Working America*.

Ravi Batra, *The Great American Deception: What Politicians Won't Tell You About Our Economy and Your Future*, New York: Wiley, 1997: a professor of international trade and economics at Southern Methodist University, Batra is particularly effective at analyzing the low economic growth of recent years, for which he lays the blame on a low-wage economy that does not tax the rich sufficiently.

Robert Eisner, *How Real Is the Federal Deficit?*, New York: Free Press, 1986: the books of this professor emeritus of economics at Northwestern University are invaluable for cutting through the rhetorical excesses of those who decry deficits and high taxes and explaining to general readers how government spending actually works.

David M. Gordon, *Fat and Mean: The Corporate Squeeze on Working Americans and the Myth of Managerial "Downsizing,"* New York: The Free Press, 1996: Gordon, professor of economics at the New School for Social Research in New York City, describes how the punitive labor relations of American business contribute to low productivity and overstaffed management.

Bennett Harrison, *Lean and Mean: The Changing Landscape of Corporate Power in the Age of Flexibility*, New York: Basic Books, 1994: a valuable analysis of how U.S. companies are restructuring themselves by relying more and more on outsourcing and subcontracting at home and abroad and implementing new restrictions on labor in order to produce higher profits.

Robert Kuttner, *Everything For Sale: The Virtues and Limits of Markets*, New York: Alfred A. Knopf, 1997: business analyst for *Business Week* and political analyst for the *Boston Globe*, Kuttner provides an incisive critique of our laissez-faire age and enumerates the many ways in which markets do not function efficiently; the book is particularly valuable for uncovering the weak points in the logic of those who believe the "free market" cures all, as well as the brittle doctrines fabricated by those who believe in a social system of "Law and Economics."

Kevin Phillips, *The Politics of Rich and Poor: Wealth and the American Electorate in the Reagan Aftermath*, New York: Random House, 1990; and *Arrogant Capital: Washington, Wall Street, and the Frustration of American Politics*, New York: Little, Brown, 1994: these popular and well-written accounts of capitalist excess and political chicanery by one of America's foremost political commentators (once conservative, now pushed by ultraconservatives and current events toward the center) provide information and analysis which will outrage even those who once approved of Bush and Reagan.

Edward N. Wolff, *Top Heavy*, New York: The New Press, 1996: one of the foremost economists in following trends in wealth and income inequality, Wolff combines information and economic modeling from many sources to arrive at a comprehensive picture of who gets the money and holds the economic assets in the United States.

Donald L. Barlett and James B. Steele, *America: What Went Wrong?*, 1992; and *America: Who Stole the Dream?*, Kansas City: Andrews and McMeel, 1996; *America: Who Really Pays the Taxes?*, New York: Simon & Schuster, 1994: among the best examples of comprehensive journalism, these works by two reporters for the *Philadelphia Inquirer* demonstrate how the changes in our political economy have come at the expense of ordinary Americans over the past two decades.

When thinking about inequality, capitalism, and the prospects for social change and democracy, historical background is indispensable; the following two books are true classics that are invaluable for understanding how economic forces are intertwined with political and social life.

Fernand Braudel, *Civilization and Capitalism* (Volumes I, II, and III), New York: Harper & Row, 1981, 1982, and 1984: deals with the emergence of the capitalist system from the fifteenth to the eighteenth centuries and manages to relate these developments to present worldwide capitalist structures. Braudel, one of the most important historians of the twentieth century, manages to capture the contradictory nature of capitalism: the energy of everyday trading and productive activity on the one hand, the oppression and inequality imposed by upper-class control over a world political economy on the other.

Howard Zinn, *A People's History of the United States*, New York: Harper & Row, 1980: the history of the U.S. told from the point of view of the common people, with an emphasis on the pattern of popular resistance to oligarchic rule, racial and sexual oppression, and economic exploitation.

The study of economics, before it was made unduly abstract, used to be called "political economy," a term which indicates that economic activity depends on political power and social-historical forces. Contemporary readers will find it worthwhile to look back to the two masterworks: Adam Smith, *The Wealth of Nations*, and Karl Marx, *Capital*.

Smith, were he alive today, would have serious moral objections to the way capitalists have increased economic inequality (and the way economists extolling his version of the "free market" glibly excuse poverty in the midst of plenty); in his 1776 book, he recognized a truth that exists to this day, that owners held a significant advantage over workers: "Many workmen could not subsist a week, few could subsist a month, and scarce any a year without employment." And while Marx was interested in theories involving the material forces of history, he was extremely well grounded in the economic realities and political events of his time. His descriptions of economic exploitation and social misery in nineteenth-century England are very instructive because they foretell the present-day conditions of work and impoverishment around the world; to a large degree, the globalization of capitalist relations is following the pattern he exposed in England.

OTHER VALUABLE SOURCES

The following books and periodicals served as valuable resources for this work and are recommended to those who want to deepen their understanding of social structures, economic conditions, politics, and history in the United States:

Albelda, Randy, Nancy Folbre, and the Center for Popular Economics, *The War on the Poor*, New York: The New Press, 1996.

Bagdikian, Ben, *The Media Monopoly*, Boston: Beacon Hill, 1987, 1990.

Barnet, Richard and John Cavanagh, *Global Dreams*, New York: Simon & Schuster, 1994.

Bluestone, Barry and Bennett Harrison, *The Deindustrialization of America*, New York: Basic Books, 1982.

———, *The Great U-Turn*, New York: Basic Books, 1988.

Brouwer, Steve, *Conquest and Capitalism, 1492–1992*, Carlisle, PA: Big Picture Books, 1992.

Brouwer, Steve, Susan D. Rose, and Paul Gifford, *Exporting the American Gospel: Global Christian Fundamentalism*, New York and London: Routledge, 1996.

Burch, Philip H., Jr., *Elites in American History* (Volumes I, II, and III), New York: Holmes and Meier, 1980.

Chomsky, Noam and Edward Herman, *Manufacturing Consent*, New York: Pantheon, 1988.

Danziger, Sheldon and Peter Gottschalk, *America Unequal*, Cambridge: Harvard University Press, 1995.

Domhoff, G. William, *Who Rules America Now?*, Englewood Cliffs, NJ: Prentice Hall, 1983.

———, *The Power Elite and the State*, New York: Aldine de Gruyter, 1990.

DuBoff, Richard R., *Accumulation and Power: An Economic History of the United States*, Armonk, NY: M.E. Sharpe, 1989.

Ehrenreich, Barbara, *Fear of Falling*, New York: Pantheon, 1989.

Faux, Jeff, *The Party's Not Over: A New Vision for the Democrats*, New York: Basic Books, 1996.

Ferguson, Thomas, *Golden Rule: the Investment Theory of Party Competition and the Logic of Money-Driven Political Systems*, Chicago: University of Chicago Press, 1995.

—— and Joel Rogers, *Right Turn: The Decline of the Democrats and the Future of American Politics*, New York: Hill and Wang, 1986.

Folbre, Nancy and the Center for Popular Economics, *A Field Guide to the U.S. Economy*, New York: The New Press, 1995.

Freeman, Richard B. and Lawrence F. Katz, eds., *Differences and Changes in Wage Structures*, Chicago: University of Chicago Press, 1995.

——and James L. Medoff, *What Do Unions Do?*, New York: Basic Books, 1984.

Galbraith, John Kenneth, *The Great Crash*, Boston: Houghton Mifflin, 1979.

Gilbert, Dennis and Joseph P. Kaul, *The American Class Structure*, Belmont, CA: Wadsworth, 1993.

Gordon, David M. and the Institute for Labor Education and Research, *What's Wrong with the U.S. Economy?*, Boston: South End Press, 1982.

Greider, William, *One World, Ready or Not*, New York: Simon & Schuster, 1997.

——*Secrets of the Temple: How the Federal Reserve Runs the Country*, New York: Simon & Schuster, 1987.

Hacker, Andrew, *Money: Who Has How Much and Why*, New York: Scribner, 1997.

Hart-Landsberg, Martin, *The Rush To Development: Economic Change and Political Struggle in South Korea*, New York: Monthly Review Press, 1993.

Henwood, Doug, *Wall Street*, London: Verso, 1997.

Herman, Edward S., *Corporate Control, Corporate Power*, New York: Cambridge University Press, 1981.

Himmelstein, David and Steffie Woolhandler, *The National Health Program Book*, Monroe, Maine: Common Courage Press, 1994.

Kolko, Joyce, *Restructuring the World Economy*, New York: Pantheon, 1988.

Krugman, Paul, *Peddling Prosperity: Economic Sense and Nonsense in the Age of Diminished Expectations*, New York: W.W. Norton, 1994.

Lapham, Lewis, *Money and Class in America*, New York: Weidenfeld and Nicolson, 1988.

Michalowski, Raymond J., *Order , Law, and Crime: An Introduction to Criminology*, New York: Random House, 1980.

Mills, C. Wright, *The Power Elite*, New York: Oxford, 1956.

Milner, Henry, *Sweden: Social Democracy in Practice*, New York: Oxford University Press, 1989.

Newman, Katharine S., *Declining Fortunes: The Withering of the American Dream*, New York: Basic Books, 1993.

Odendahl, Teresa, *Charity Begins at Home: Generosity and Self-Interest among the Philanthropic Elite*, New York: Basic Books, 1990.

Parenti, Michael, *Democracy for the Few*, New York: Random House, 1982.

Phillips, Kevin, *Post-Conservative America*, New York: Random House, 1982.

Piven, Frances Fox and Richard Cloward, *The New Class War*, New York: Pantheon, 1982.

Reich, Robert, *The Work of Nations*, New York: Knopf, 1991.

Rose, Stephen J., *The American Profile Poster*, New York: Pantheon, 1986.

Sidel, Ruth, *Women and Children Last*, New York: Viking, 1986.

Schor, Juliet, *The Overworked American*, New York: Basic Books, 1992.

Schwartz, John E. and Thomas J. Volgy, *The Forgotten Americans*, New York: W.W. Norton, 1992.

Thurow, Lester, *Head to Head: The Coming Battle Among Japan, Europe, and America*, New York: William Morrow, 1992.

Wilson, William Julius, *When Work Disappears: The World of the New Urban Poor*, New York: Alfred A. Knopf, 1996.

Wright, Erik Olin, *Class Counts: Comparative Studies in Class Analysis*, New York: Cambridge University Press, 1996.

Wright Erik Olin, *Classes*, London: New Left Books, 1985.

RECOMMENDED PERIODICALS AND NEWSPAPERS:

Business Week
Challenge
Dollars and Sense
Economic Notes
The Economist
Far Eastern Economic Review
Forbes
Fortune
In These Times
Left Business Observer
Monthly Review
The Nation
The New York Times
The Progressive
Social Policy
U.S. News & World Report
The Wall Street Journal
The Washington Post

GOVERNMENT SOURCE MATERIALS:

Economic Indicators, prepared for the Joint Economic Committee by the Council of Economic Advisors, Washington, D.C.: U.S. Government Printing Office.

OECD (Organization for Economic Co-operation and Development), various publications.

U.S. Department of Labor, Bureau of Statistics, *Employment and Earnings*, Washington, D.C.: U.S. Government Printing Office.

Index